Cambridge

MW00640505

Elements in the Philosophy of Ludwig Wittgenstein
edited by
David G. Stern
University of Iowa

WITTGENSTEIN ON REALISM AND IDEALISM

David R. Cerbone
West Virginia University

CAMBRIDGE
UNIVERSITY PRESS

Shaftesbury Road, Cambridge CB2 8EA, United Kingdom

One Liberty Plaza, 20th Floor, New York, NY 10006, USA

477 Williamstown Road, Port Melbourne, VIC 3207, Australia

314–321, 3rd Floor, Plot 3, Splendor Forum, Jasola District Centre, New Delhi – 110025, India

103 Penang Road, #05–06/07, Visioncrest Commercial, Singapore 238467

Cambridge University Press is part of Cambridge University Press & Assessment, a department of the University of Cambridge.

We share the University's mission to contribute to society through the pursuit of education, learning and research at the highest international levels of excellence.

www.cambridge.org
Information on this title: www.cambridge.org/9781009475631

DOI: 10.1017/9781108920766

First published 2023

A catalogue record for this publication is available from the British Library.

ISBN 978-1-009-47563-1 Hardback
ISBN 978-1-108-82702-7 Paperback
ISSN 2632-7112 (online)
ISSN 2632-7104 (print)

Wittgenstein on Realism and Idealism

Elements in the Philosophy of Ludwig Wittgenstein

DOI: 10.1017/9781108920766
First published online: December 2023

David R. Cerbone
West Virginia University
Author for correspondence: David R Cerbone, dcerbone@mail.wvu.edu

Abstract: This Element concerns Wittgenstein's evolving attitude toward the opposition between realism and idealism in philosophy. Despite the marked – and sometimes radical – changes Wittgenstein's thinking undergoes from the early to the middle to the later period, there is an underlying continuity in terms of his unwillingness at any point to endorse either position in a straightforward manner. Instead, Wittgenstein can be understood as rejecting both positions, while nonetheless seeing insights in each position worth retaining. The author traces these "neither-nor" and "both-and" strands of Wittgenstein's attitude toward realism and idealism to his – again, evolving – insistence on seeing language and thought as worldly phenomena. That thought and language are about the world and happen amidst the world they are about undermines the attempt to formulate any kind of general thesis concerning their interrelation.

Keywords: Wittgenstein, realism, idealism, philosophical method, quietism

ISBNs: 9781009475631 (HB), 9781108827027 (PB), 9781108920766 (OC)
ISSNs: 2632-7112 (online), 2632-7104 (print)

Contents

Introduction

This Element concerns Wittgenstein's philosophy in relation to realism and idealism. Before offering a preliminary sketch of Wittgenstein's attitude toward realism and idealism – and what I take to be distinctive about it – I want to say something about the targets of that attitude. An immediate difficulty in doing so is that neither *-ism* denotes a single, clearly demarcated position to which Wittgenstein's philosophy can be clearly or univocally related. Nietzsche notoriously wrote that "only something which has no history is capable of being defined." While we perhaps do not need to go quite that far, I think it is safe to say that both *realism* and *idealism* have very long histories and so, like many central terms in the history of philosophy, resist any kind of concise definition. Despite the risk of oversimplification, we can get a feel for what realism and idealism – and their opposition – are all about by noting character-izations offered by both G. E. Moore and Bertrand Russell. These characteriza-tions have the added benefit of being offered by figures with whom Wittgenstein had close relationships. In his 1903 paper, "The Refutation of Idealism," Moore succinctly characterizes idealism in the following terms: "Modern idealism, if it asserts any general conclusion about the world at all, asserts that it is *spiritual*" (Moore, 1959, 1). Notice that Moore's formulation casts idealism as an *onto-logical* thesis about *what there is* or what the world is *made of*. Despite Moore's ascribing this ontology to modern idealism in general, it does not accommodate comfortably one of its most prominent adherents, namely, Kant: in drawing the limits to reason, Kant's critical philosophy forbids general theses about what there is, as that would pertain to things-in-themselves rather than *appearances*. While also commendably terse, Russell's characterization allows for this epis-temological dimension of idealism. Noting that "the word 'idealism' is used by different philosophers in somewhat different senses," Russell describes the doctrine as holding that "whatever exists, or at any rate whatever can be known to exist, must be in some sense mental" (Russell, 1959, 37).[1]

In their succinctness, these formulations from Russell and Moore neglect the myriad forms of idealism whose variety is signaled by the variety of modifiers that may be added to the term: *empirical* idealism, *transcendental* idealism, and *absolute* idealism, for example, are all very different views, as opposed to one another as to various forms of realism. So there is nothing like idealism *as such* that can be uncontroversially delineated and evaluated in relation to realism *as*

---

[1] On the subsequent page, Russell more fully acknowledges Kantian idealism, albeit without mentioning Kant by name: "The grounds on which idealism is advocated are generally grounds derived from a theory of knowledge, that is to say, from a discussion of the conditions which things must satisfy in order that we may be able to know them" (38).

such. There is a further complexity when weighing in on these topics owing to another variety of modifier or qualifier that often accompanies *realism* more so than idealism. These qualifiers restrict the area of concern in some way, to a particular range of concepts or a particular kind of inquiry. There are protracted debates in philosophy on such topics as *moral* realism, *mathematical* realism, and *scientific* realism where what fuels those debates are concerns specific to the domain in question. To some philosophers, *values* do not look to be the kind of thing that populate the world in the way that squirrels and trees do; things (if they are indeed *things*) like *numbers* and *sets* look kind of odd too; and while the oddity of the first two is often measured against the "hard" reality of things like protons and electrons, opponents to scientific realism see such things' unobservability as warranting caution when it comes to believing in them. Yet a further complicating factor here is that such qualified forms of realism tend to be opposed not so much by idealism as by *anti-realism*, where there is at least a serious question of how such positions line up with idealism. If, for example, anti-realism denies the (full or objective) reality of something because it is *socially constructed*, that does not comport – or at least does not comport automatically – with more traditional forms of idealism and its emphasis on ideas, appearances, and other things spiritual.

We can perhaps sidestep some of these difficulties by primarily attending to what Wittgenstein himself says about realism and idealism to gain a sense of how he understands the positions, what is at stake in thinking about them, and what his attitude toward the two positions and their interplay ultimately is. Once all of this has been worked out, we can then take a step back and determine how these bear upon our own commitments when it comes to realism and idealism (including what those commitments ought to be). We can call this sort of approach an inside-out strategy, as we start from within Wittgenstein's writings and work our way out toward conclusions about realism and idealism. This strategy can be contrasted with an approach that proceeds in the opposite direction, starting from a consideration of the issue of realism and idealism – their respective commitments and liabilities, strengths and weaknesses – and then approaching Wittgenstein's texts with an eye toward determining the extent to which they incur those commitments or liabilities. While this sort of outside-in strategy may attend to passages where Wittgenstein explicitly mentions realism or idealism (or both – more on that momentarily), they need not figure centrally in the overall evaluation of Wittgenstein's philosophy. (This is especially evident in many of the interpretations of the later work as committed to some form of idealism.)

There are merits and shortcomings to both approaches. While the inside-out approach has the virtue of being especially sensitive and attentive to what

Wittgenstein himself says about realism and idealism, his own understanding of these ideas might be seen as rather narrow and idiosyncratic. This is especially worrisome in his handling of *idealism*, which he often lumps together with *solipsism*.[2] While this tendency is most prominent in the early period, the middle period's interest in "phenomenology" and the idea of a language that describes my "immediate experience" maintains a close connection between idealism and solipsism: to be an idealist is to be committed to the primacy of my awareness of my immediate experience (my awareness of *appearances*).[3] Given this basic commitment, it is a short step from idealism to solipsism, from *primacy* to *exclusivity*, as it is not clear how my "awareness" ever gets any further. While this is a recognizable form of idealism, it is but one variety and a fairly crude one at that. One need only look to Kant's philosophy to enlarge one's perspective on idealism, as the *Critique of Pure Reason* purports to offer a "refutation" of just this sort of idealism – what Kant refers to as *empirical idealism* – while itself developing a more sophisticated – and, Kant thinks, less problematic – form of idealism (*transcendental* rather than empirical idealism).[4] One can ask, for example, if Wittgenstein is committed to some form of transcendental idealism, as many readers have done; settling this question will not be furthered all that much by appealing to passages where Wittgenstein discusses and perhaps quite explicitly rejects idealism in its more solipsistic varieties (such rejections are fully compatible with a commitment – unwittingly or not – to a more Kantian variety of idealism).

There are likewise merits and shortcomings to a more outside-in strategy. Apart from the danger of never getting to what Wittgenstein actually says or thinks owing to the variety of positions that might be staked out across a wide array of domains, there is also the risk of distorting – or just missing – what is distinctive about Wittgenstein's philosophy. What I mean here is that the outside-in strategy encourages a desire to find in Wittgenstein's work some kind of more or less sophisticated philosophical thesis or theory – some form of realism or idealism suitably modified and qualified, for example – whose strengths and weaknesses might then be determined. Approaches of this kind often ignore – or explain away – Wittgenstein's own characterizations of what he is up to or what he is after. They do not, among other things, take seriously (or seriously enough) Wittgenstein's remarks about progress in philosophy: at the

---

[2] See Ritter (2020), chapter 2 for a discussion of the relation between Wittgenstein's discussions of idealism and attributions to him of more sophisticated forms of idealism.

[3] See chapter 5 of Stern (1995) for an account of Wittgenstein's interest in – and later disenchantment with – the notion of immediate experience.

[4] See Ritter (2020) for a nuanced discussion of Kant's refutation of idealism in relation to Wittgenstein's middle and later philosophy.

close of the Preface to the *Tractatus*, he notes "how little is achieved" when the problems of philosophy are solved; such an attitude persists into the *Investigations*, as the motto from Nestroy suggests.[5] Nor do such approaches take seriously (or seriously enough) Wittgenstein's own disclaimers and disavowals when it comes to theories and theses. With that much philosophical writing – peculiar looking though it is – there has got to be a theory or two in there somewhere!

The liabilities of approaching Wittgenstein with an eye toward ascribing to him some form of realism or idealism can be made more evident by further attending to the inside-out strategy. I will do so at considerable length throughout this Element, but I'll offer an overview here. There are references to realism and idealism scattered throughout Wittgenstein's writings ranging from his wartime notebooks of 1914–16 to his writings of the "middle period" of the 1930s and into the later work all the way to his last remarks collected in *On Certainty*. An archival search[6] yields forty-nine occurrences of *Idealismus* and thirty-one for *Realismus* (searches that include variants on these core terms yield even more). Most of the *Nachlass* remarks are in the writings of the 1930s: there are numerous references in *Philosophical Remarks* and surrounding manuscripts and typescripts, and *The Big Typescript* contains an entire section entitled "Idealism." There are, however, no references to realism and idealism in the *Philosophical Investigations*;[7] we find only a reference to the *adherents* espousing such views rather than to the views themselves, in the second paragraph of § 402: "For *this* is what disputes between idealists, solipsists, and realists look like. The one party attacks the normal form of expression as if they were attacking an assertion; the others defend it, as if they were stating facts recognized by every reasonable human being" (PI, § 402).

While simple arithmetic shows that Wittgenstein does not *always* refer to realism and idealism together, as the number of references to idealism overall is significantly larger than references to realism, this singular appearance in the *Investigations* is illustrative of a recurring theme in Wittgenstein's references to realism and idealism: when he refers to them together, he does so not to choose sides, but to treat them as two sides of one problematic coin. That is,

---

[5] The motto reads: "The trouble about progress is that it always looks much greater than it really is."

[6] Using http://wittfind.cis.uni-muenchen.de.

[7] This fade-out should not be construed as an abandonment of the concerns that animate Wittgenstein's more extended discussions of realism and idealism. That Wittgenstein notes in the mid-1940s that his thoughts about idealism and solipsism "hang together" with the "possibility of a 'private language'" registers the ongoing significance of his engagement with realism and idealism. See BNE, MS-124, 188[6] et189[1].

Wittgenstein is often interested in the dispute between realism and idealism not as something to be settled in favor of one side or the other, but as instructive for understanding how philosophical confusions arise and how they might ultimately be clarified.

One aim of this Element is to illustrate the pervasiveness of this kind of attitude toward realism and idealism, from Wittgenstein's earliest writings all the way to the end of his life.[8] Indeed, in a letter to Mary Elwyn in 1966, Rush Rhees recounts Wittgenstein's first meeting with Bertrand Russell (Wittgenstein at the time was still a student at Manchester Technical College; a mentor there had encouraged him to read Russell's *The Principles of Mathematics*). In response to a remark made by Russell "against idealism," Wittgenstein "replied that he did not think either realism or idealism was satisfactory: one would have to take some third position between them." Russell replied that an intermediate position "would not help," as "you would have to have an intermediate position between this new one and each of the others, and so on ad infinitum" (Rhees 2015, 50).[9] Clearly Wittgenstein's desire to avoid identifying with either realism or idealism runs deep. This kind of desire is evident throughout Wittgenstein's remarks on realism and idealism, as these representative samples (listed in chronological order) attest:

> This is the way I have travelled: Idealism singles men out from the world as unique, solipsism singles me alone out, and at last I see that I too belong with the rest of the world, and so on the one side *nothing* is left over, and on the other side, *the world*. In this way idealism leads to realism if it is strictly thought out. (NB, 85)[10]

> From the very outset "Realism," "Idealism," etc., are names which belong to metaphysics. That is, they indicate that their adherents believe they can say something specific about the essence of the world. (PR, § 55)

> Realism is always right in what it says. But idealism sees problems that are there and that realism does not see. (BNE, MS-156b, 22 v)[11]

These passages will be given due consideration in what follows, but for now I want to emphasize the way they indicate Wittgenstein's interest in the interplay between realism and idealism, but, beyond that, the different ways that interplay might be understood. The *Investigations* passage suggests that idealism and realism look to be locked in a kind of dispute, where their respective

---

[8] Such inner consistency is a central theme of Bartmann (2021).
[9] I am grateful to David Devalle for bringing this passage to my attention.
[10] This passage anticipates TLP 5.64, which will be discussed at length in Section 1.
[11] Ritter (2020) notes the importance of this passage. I am also grateful to Alois Pichler, whose correspondence prompted me to think harder about this particular remark.

adherents are entering opposing claims. The passage further suggests that the dispute is only *apparent* – indicated by Wittgenstein's "as if" – such that there are not really opposing *theses* at all. The passage from *Philosophical Remarks* likewise suggests that realism and idealism both succumb to a kind of illusion. Wittgenstein's labeling realism and idealism as "names which belong to metaphysics" is hardly a ringing endorsement – indeed, quite the opposite – and the tone of the passage conveys an attitude of skepticism toward what "adherents" to such views "believe they can say," namely "something specific about the essence of the world." Just where and how such beliefs misfire will need to be explored, but for now, I note only that the passage from the *Remarks*, like the passage from the *Investigations*, displays a kind of neither-nor attitude toward realism and idealism, where each falls prey to an illusion whose form is common to both sides.

The early remark from the *Notebooks* and the manuscript remark from the 1930s work differently, in that neither of them offers a flatly neither-nor outlook. There is in each of them a kind of endorsement of realism: realism is a kind of "final destination" in the early remark and Wittgenstein declares the realist to be "always right" in the manuscript remark.[12] Neither of the passages, however, offers a simple endorsement of realism and in ways that I think are related to one another, despite the distance between the *Notebooks* remark and the manuscript remark from the 1930s. A lot hangs here on just what kind of "problems" idealism sees that the realist fails to notice, but these problems are described as really being there (they are not merely apparent in the manner of logical positivism's pseudo-problems). This suggests that the idealist is on to something that a simple endorsement of realism obscures or covers over. The idea that the idealist is on to something is likewise indicated in the passage from Wittgenstein's wartime notebooks, which anticipates his talk in the *Tractatus* of solipsism coinciding with "pure realism" (TLP 5.64). Whatever Wittgenstein ultimately means here – more attention will be given to these ideas shortly – I think we can safely say that there is something to be gained in traveling, as Wittgenstein describes himself in the notebook passage, from idealism to solipsism to realism (the suggestion of a journey is retained in the *Tractatus'* talk of *following out* the implications of solipsism), where the "journey" is not to be understood solely as a passage from incorrect views to the correct one, such

[12] To these we can add Wittgenstein's remark: "Not empiricism and yet realism in philosophy, that is the hardest thing" (RFM VI, § 23). This remark is central to Cora Diamond's reading of Wittgenstein as exemplifying a "realistic spirit." See the essays contained in Diamond (1991), especially "Realism and the Realistic Spirit." See also chapter 7 of Cockburn (2021) for extended reflection on realism and idealism starting from this remark. The general direction of Cockburn's thinking seems to me to be consonant with the interpretation of Wittgenstein pursued in this Element.

that one would be better off just starting at the journey's end. Rather, something is learned – and retained – by tracing the path from one to another: we learn something in seeing – and seeing *how* – solipsism and realism "coincide." The journey brings into view the kinds of problems the later manuscript passage mentions that realism by itself leaves obscured. There is thus across these remarks a sense of idealism as involving a kind of insight that needs to be worried over – and preserved – despite realism's basic correctness. Rather than a neither-nor dismissal of realism and idealism, we see instead a kind of both-and attitude that accords to each side at least some merit.

Wittgenstein's ambivalence about realism and idealism – his oscillation between neither-nor and both-and attitudes – accords with his reluctance to offer – or endorse – any particular philosophical thesis. His ambivalence further accords with the way Wittgenstein is working at a more basic, but for that reason also more elusive, level, where "realism" and "idealism," as well as "realism about . . ." and "anti-realism about . . .," begin to get a foothold in our thinking. In his later philosophy especially, Wittgenstein characterizes his activity as directed not so much to worked-out philosophical views (he rarely "names names" or considers other people's work in a sustained way) as much as to what he calls *pictures*. Saying just what Wittgenstein means by a picture (which is not to be confused with his interest in picturing in his early philosophy) is by no means easy, but we can think of it as involving largely unnoticed assumptions, presuppositions, and commitments that precede and inform explicit philosophical inquiry.[13] Such explicit philosophical inquiry carries on its activities – constructing arguments, refining positions, shuttling between point and counterpoint – in ways that might *feel* substantive and yet be liable to implosion were only those largely unnoticed assumptions, presuppositions, and commitments brought into view and interrogated more directly. Wittgenstein's philosophy – especially the later philosophy centered on the *Philosophical Investigations* – is taken up with the latter kind of interrogation, which is part of why his texts look so puzzling – and are often so annoying – to so many trained philosophers.

To get a feel for the kind of picture in play here, consider a very traditional formulation of the notion of *truth* – and, by extension, the notion of *knowledge* – which can be found in the work of St. Thomas Aquinas: *Adaequatio rei et intellectus*, the "adequation" of things and intellect. This formulation recurs throughout later philosophy, for example in Kant and Heidegger. The formula presents us with a kind of fundamental division, between what is referred to here just as "things" and the "intellect." The two are depicted as separate from one

---

[13] The idea that Wittgenstein is operating on a proto-philosophical level is central to Goldfarb (1983).

another and yet capable of standing in a relation of "adequation." The *direction* of that relation is left open in the formulation, but I think it is most natural to think of it like this: there is a way things are and there are things going on in the intellect. What is going on in the intellect counts as *true* – is a candidate for *knowledge* – where what is going on in the intellect is *adequate* to the way things are. I think to myself, "The book I want to read is on the coffee table in the living room." I proceed downstairs to the living room: lo and behold, no book on the coffee table. In this case, what I had thought – that the book is on the coffee table – did not line up with, was not adequate to, how things are in the living room. While there is something natural or intuitive about this way of understanding the direction of adequation, Kant, among others, thought that if we really think these ideas through, we will come to see that they make knowledge impossible. That is, if we take seriously that *we* occupy the perspective of "the intellect," then determining the adequation between what is in the intellect and things beyond the intellect would require occupying a position *outside* the intellect. Only in such a way could the extent of adequation – the extent of its success or failure – be determined. Such a "sideways-on" perspective is precisely what is *not* available to us insofar as our own intellects are at issue.[14] Once I grasp that the mind is that through which I grasp anything at all, then grasp of anything without the mind (in both senses of "without") starts to look impossible. The Kantian proposal in the face of this seeming impossibility is to reverse the direction: rather than the mind making itself adequate – or conforming itself – to things, we are instead to consider only the ways in which things make themselves adequate – or conform themselves – to the basic structures of the intellect: things will be *knowable* – although not always *known* – just insofar as they adhere to those structures.

This is an admittedly crude sketch of the ways one might start spelling out the idea of adequation. What is important for my purposes, in accordance with what I said earlier about Wittgenstein and pictures, is the basic presuppositions of the formulation, regardless of which "direction" gets emphasized. Most fundamentally, we start from an idea of the intellect or mind, on the one hand, and an idea of things, on the other. There is a way things are with (or in) the intellect and a way things are apart from the intellect: mind and world, thought and reality. Both realism and idealism, I want to suggest, start from this fundamental

---

[14] That Wittgenstein's philosophy is directed toward the confusions that attend aspiring to a sideways-on perspective on our relation to the world has long been a central theme in the work of John McDowell. See, most notably, McDowell (1996). The reading of Wittgenstein that I offer in this Element very much gibes with his criticisms of anti-realist readings of Wittgenstein, especially in their desire to locate "sub-'bedrock'" resources to account for understanding and meaning in some more basic terms. See McDowell (1984), especially § 11.

separation, this divide between what pertains to the intellect and what pertains to reality. Rejecting this separation involves some kind of concession to the realist, as the thesis that reality is mind-dependent fails to get a foothold. At the same time, Wittgenstein's insistence that idealism is on to something is apt to look suspicious to the committed realist. The real challenge – implicit in Russell's warning to the young Wittgenstein – is to dissolve the opposition between realism and idealism rather than find an intermediate position, some further thesis that sets out *the* relation between mind and world. In *The Big Typescript*, Wittgenstein writes parenthetically: "All that philosophy can do is to destroy idols. And that means not creating a new one – say in the 'absence of an idol'" (BT, 305). The challenge here is one of destroying an idol without thereby leaving, as it were, an idol-shaped hole.

To offer one final introductory sketch of Wittgenstein's perspective on realism and idealism, I want to consider what I take to be an emblematic remark. The passage has a curiously dogged but unstable persistence in Wittgenstein's writings. A version of the passage first appears in TS-211 from the early 1930s; pieces of it resurface in both *Philosophical Grammar* and *The Big Typescript*; and versions of it appear in four further typescripts, the last three of which are from 1945. The passage can also be found in *Philosophical Investigations* amidst the remarks from the early 100s devoted primarily to Wittgenstein's reflections on his own procedures and aims. However, the passage does not belong to the sequence of numbered remarks, but instead appears as a boxed remark between § 108 and § 109. According to Hacker and Schulte's notes for the most recent edition of the *Investigations*, the passage was printed as paragraphs (b) to (d) of § 108 in the first two editions, but its source is "a handwritten note on a slip of paper, inserted between pp. 82 and 83 of TSS 227." They add that "there is no clear indication as to where exactly to place it" (PI, Notes, 253). The longevity of the remark attests to its importance to Wittgenstein; that he never settled on where to place it in the sequence of remarks in the *Investigations* can perhaps be understood as further underscoring its significance. What I mean here is that the ideas expressed in this passage are *so* fundamental and pervasive as to preclude finding a singular (let alone obvious) place to situate it.

Here is the *Investigations* version of the passage:

> The sense in which philosophy of logic speaks of sentences and words is no different from that in which we speak of them in ordinary life when we say, for example, "What is written here is a Chinese sentence," or "No, that only looks like writing; it's actually just ornamental," and so on.
>
> We're talking about the spatial and temporal phenomenon of language, not about some non-spatial, atemporal non-entity. [Only it is possible to be

interested in a phenomenon in a variety of ways]. But we talk about it as we
do about the pieces in chess when we are stating the rules for their moves, not
describing their physical properties.
    The question "What is a word really?" is analogous to "What is a piece in
chess?"

There is a lot to sort through in these three short paragraphs, but I want here to
call attention only to the first sentence of the second paragraph. I read
Wittgenstein's insistence on talking about language as a "spatial and temporal
phenomenon" as bearing upon the viability of the kind of separation between
mind and world that funds both idealist and realist points of view. Wittgenstein's
insistence is upon understanding language (and thought – §109 targets what he
refers to there as a "pneumatic conception of thinking") as a *worldly phenomenon*. The sense of *worldly* can be further unpacked in two ways, in accordance
with two ways of understanding how language is *of* the world:

i. Language and thought are fundamentally *of* the world in the sense of being
    about the world
ii. Language and thought are fundamentally *of* the world in the sense of
    belonging to (or *happening within*) the world (they are about)

The first of these predominates in the early work's understanding of language
and thought in terms of *pictorial representation* (the so-called picture theory).
For the early Wittgenstein, the very idea of a proposition – of a meaningful
move in language and thought – is world-involving: its meaning consists in its
depicting the world *as* being some way rather than another. (That language is
applied to the world is misleading at best, as it suggests that a conception of
language can be made out apart from its bearing upon the world.) I'll argue later
(Section 2.1) that Wittgenstein's pictorial conception of propositions is key to
his enigmatic claim that solipsism and realism coincide. While more muted,
I think the second sense is present already in the *Tractatus* and in a number of
ways: language belongs to the world insofar as pictures are themselves *facts* (if
the world, as the opening remarks of the *Tractatus* have it, is "the totality of
facts," then propositions as themselves facts belong to that totality). But there
are suggestions of the worldly character of language in the further sense of being
"a spatial and temporal phenomenon" at various points in the *Tractatus*. That we
make pictures calls attention to the practical dimensions of language, as does the
way Wittgenstein's distinction between *sign* and *symbol* turns on the *use* of
signs (a harbinger of § 43 of the *Investigations*). Moreover, at other places in the
Tractatus, he associates language (and its complexity) with the human organism, which again underscores how we represent the world from within the world
we so represent.

In the middle and later work, the first of these two senses of *of the world* becomes more muted, although it does not disappear from view entirely. In *Philosophical Remarks*, for example, he writes: "For since language only derives the way in which it means from its meaning, from the world, no language is conceivable which does not represent the world" (PR, § 47). One thing we do with language is represent the world – say how things are – but that is only one way we use language, one aspect of language use. The way in which the first sense of *of the world* becomes muted indicates the ways in which the second sense gains prominence: the sense of language as belonging to the world becomes increasingly *pluralized* and *naturalized*. The notion of pluralization emerges as a theme in *Philosophical Remarks*, in which Wittgenstein revisits – and reconfigures – the sense-nonsense distinction in ways that move against the kind of monolithic account of language one finds in the *Tractatus*. In *Philosophical Grammar*, we again see this kind of pluralization, now woven together with a sense of life itself as multifarious and complicated: "Well language does connect up with my own life. And what is called 'language' is something made up of heterogeneous elements and the way it meshes with life is infinitely various" (PG, 66).

Heterogeneity and the living character of language are also prominent themes in *Philosophical Investigations*, as early as § 7, where Wittgenstein introduces the notion of *language-games*: in addition to emphasizing their plurality, his final remark in the passage calls attention to "the whole, consisting of language and the activities into which it is woven." Language as a "spatial and temporal phenomenon" is bound up with the spatial and temporal activities of our lives. It is in this way a part of our "natural history" (see PI, § 25). I'll argue that this kind of natural historical perspective is at odds with – and undermines – any kind of *general* thesis along the lines of realism or idealism.

1 The Early Wittgenstein

The very first words of Wittgenstein's first numbered proposition in the *Tractatus* – the first of the seven principal remarks upon which all the rest function as layered commentary – are *the world*.[15] Immediately prior to the closing proposition and its invocation of silence, and immediately following 6.54's image of throwing away the ladder one has climbed by working through the *Tractatus*, Wittgenstein describes the results of that climb as a matter of "seeing the world aright." So what starts by putting the world front and center, but also at the bottom "rung" of the ladder we then begin to climb, ends with the

---

[15] The revelation of the world is a central emphasis of Friedlander (2001).

enlightened reader perched atop wherever this climb has brought her/him having the world even more clearly in view than at the outset. Since the reader has not been stationary between the first proposition and the closing remarks, at some points along the way the view of the world will likely have been obscured in some way or another. That is, there are rungs on the ladder that withdraw us from the world or threaten to distort our perspective on it, so that we do not see it "aright." This withdrawal of the world from view is most pronounced late in the 5s, where solipsism is raised as a temptation; only when solipsism is seen to "coincide" with "pure realism" does the world come back into view and the climb continue. There are thus elements of the *Tractatus* that invite the charge of idealism – that make idealism seem inevitable – only to return us to the reality of the world.[16]

I will not in this section be able to review the entire "climb" from the first proposition of the *Tractatus* to the point where solipsism comes into view, but only those "rungs" that seem to me to bear most directly on our arriving at solipsism as an issue in the 5s. The points along the climb that lead us to solipsism that I want to emphasize are those places where Wittgenstein talks about *pictures* and *picturing*.[17] While the emphasis in the initial exposition of pictures and picturing is clearly world-oriented – we make pictures *of* the world using worldly elements – there are questions that arise about picturing that point in a more idealistic direction.[18] There is something right in this, but also

---

[16] There are many ways to approach the issue of realism and idealism in the *Tractatus*. One way is via Moore and Russell's earlier "revolt against idealism" in favor of a kind of realism. See Bartmann (2021) for an insightful and illuminating example of this approach. Bartmann places considerable emphasis on Wittgenstein's critique of Russell's conception of judgment and the problem of the unity of the proposition. Another is to interrogate the status of "objects" in the *Tractatus* and his identification of them as the "substance" of the world (see 2.021). How are we to understand such objects? Can they be identified or associated with anything we might identify by other means, such as physical atoms or mentally inflected sense data? How one answers this last question suggests a different verdict in terms of the *Tractatus* having a "realist ontology" or an "idealist ontology." See McGuinness (1981) and Ishiguro (1969); and again, see Bartmann (2021), especially chapter 3, for review and assessment of the issue. Bartmann rightly rejects an objects-first approach to the *Tractatus*, as it misses entirely the way "logic pervades the world." Despite his overall interest in Wittgenstein's stance on realism and idealism – what he refers to as Wittgenstein's "metametaphysics" – Bartmann does not consider the passages in the *Tractatus* that explicitly address their coincidence via reflection on solipsism.

[17] In thinking about the *Tractatus*, pictures, and picturing, I have benefited greatly from McManus (2006). My own extended example is inspired at least in part by the adventures of his pepper pot named Frank. I have also profited greatly from Sullivan (2001). Without claiming any of the depth or rigor of Sullivan's account, what I offer here accords at least with the spirit of it, exemplified in the following: "The idea that we might be thinking and yet failing to present a possible state of affairs simply gets no grip on Wittgenstein's theory: what defines the possibilities of how things might be defines also the possibilities in, that is, what constitutes, thought" (100). See also the second chapter of Proops (2000).

[18] Although I will not address this in what follows, I'm inclined to think that this line of questioning is at least part of what is at issue in the debate in Moore and Sullivan (2003) over the place of

something problematic.[19] Disentangling the correct from the confused brings us back to realism, but in a more enlightened way.

1.1 Pictures and Picturing

Wittgenstein first invokes the idea of *pictures* at 2.1: *Wir machen uns Bilder der Tatsachen* ("We make for ourselves pictures of facts"). In the Pears–McGuinness translation, *machen … Bilder* is translated with "picture" as a verb.[20] The idea of *making* (or *picturing*) is important – indeed crucial – as it calls attention to the *activity* of depicting the world. Although talk of pictures brings to mind primarily images (drawings, photographs, paintings), Wittgenstein's conception encompasses a far broader range of representations. Indeed, we are liable to miss what is essential about pictures and picturing if we stay too close to what first comes to mind,[21] as we are apt to think that what is most important about pictures is that they *look like* whatever it is they depict. While a picture's looking like what it depicts can be important in some cases – as when we talk approvingly of a portrait as being a good likeness – it is in no way essential to representations at such. This will be especially clear when Wittgenstein appeals to pictures and picturing in connection with propositions (*Satze*), but it is evident as well in his examples of musical scores and the grooves of a phonograph record: both of these are intimately related to audible music, but neither of them "look like" that audible music; indeed, talk of *looking like* is out of place, as we are comparing visible arrangements of notes and both visible and tangible grooves to something that is only heard and not seen or touched. Wittgenstein makes this clear later, at 4.011.

Almost immediately after introducing the notion of pictures and picturing, Wittgenstein glosses pictures in terms of *models*: "A picture is a model of reality" (TLP 2.12). He then introduces the idea of *elements* – "In a picture objects have the elements of the picture corresponding to them" (2.13) – and the relations among those elements: "What constitutes a picture is that its elements are related to one another in a determinate way" (2.14). He then adds that

---

transcendental idealism in the *Tractatus*. The debate is complicated, as evidenced by the parties to the debate's difficulties in spelling out just where the disagreement lies. My sense, though, is that the questions about the possibility of meaning that appear to lead to solipsism are what lead Moore in turn to see a kind of ineffable idealism lurking in the *Tractatus*.

[19] Despite the debt to McManus (2006) that I noted in footnote 17, I suspect that I am a bit more sympathetic to the appeal to *mystery* when it comes to questions about meaning than McManus is, as his account seeks to expose such lines of questioning as simply confused. See chapter 8, especially § 8.5.

[20] Richter (2022) translates 2.1 as I do.

[21] Consider TLP 4.016, where Wittgenstein cites hieroglyphic script as a more literal kind of picturing. He then notes how alphabetic script "developed out of it without losing what is essential to depiction."

"a picture is a fact" (2.141). To get a feel for what Wittgenstein is up to here, it might help to consider an example. At 3.1431, he writes regarding the propositional sign:

> The essence of a propositional sign is very clearly seen if we imagine one composed of spatial objects (such as tables, chairs, and books) instead of written signs.
>
> Then the spatial arrangement of these things will express the sense of the proposition.

Suppose I'm visiting a friend who has never visited me where I live in West Virginia and she asks me to give her a sense of what it's like. One thing I might want to emphasize – especially if I'm visiting a friend in a big city – is just how sparsely populated it is where I live and just how spread out everything is. Of course, given the ubiquity of high-speed internet (I'm in a big city in this example after all), I would most likely pull up Google Earth and show my friend an overhead view of my homestead (there's no point using the Street View setting, as we'd only maybe catch a glimpse of our mailbox up by the road). If we somehow do not have internet access, I could sketch a map with pencil and paper. But doing things this way does not hew to Wittgenstein's suggestion. Since tables and chairs are a bit cumbersome to arrange and rearrange, suppose instead that I reach for a bag of marbles that my friend happens to have handy. There's nothing special about marbles, but two things about the marbles are worth emphasizing. First, there are a number of them. One marble alone would not do the trick, nor, as we will see, would just two: "In a proposition there must be exactly as many distinguishable parts as in the situation that it represents" (TLP 4.04). Second, the marbles must be able to be arranged and rearranged, and *how* they are arranged and rearranged matters:

> A proposition is not a medley of words. – (Just as a theme in music is not a medley of notes.)
>
> A proposition is articulated. (TLP 3.141)

Piled into the bag, the marbles do not *mean* anything; there is nothing about their arrangement that stands in any kind of relationship to anything else. Notice what happens, though, when I start to take the marbles out and arrange them for my friend. I might pick up the first marble, lay it down on the coffee table while saying, "Okay, here's my house." The marble now *stands for something*, namely, my house. Of course, it does not look like my house, which is square and mostly opaque except for the windows; my house is white with a green roof and shutters, but the marble could be any color at all and still go proxy for my house in the model I'm building for my friend. So far, I have only designated the one marble as standing for my house, but I have not yet *said* anything about my house or where I live because the one marble is not yet related to anything else. I need some more marbles, so I pull out another one and place it a few inches away from the first marble: "Here's where Jimmy Snyder lives, about a half-mile south of my house." I then take out a third marble and place it around the same distance away from the second marble: "Here's the gas station, which is a further half-mile south." In contrast to the marbles when they were piled into the bag, there is now something significant about the way the three I've pulled out are arranged. The marbles are arranged in a determinate way, quite unlike how things would be if I had just pulled a handful out and let them roll around on the floor. The way the marbles are arranged is itself a fact, but it *represents* another (possible) fact in virtue of the relation between how the marbles are arranged and how things are back home in West Virginia.

> The fact that the elements of a picture are related to one another in a determinate way represents that things are related to one another in the same way.
>
> Let us call this connection of its elements the structure of the picture, and let us call the possibility of this structure the pictorial form of the picture. (TLP 2.15)
>
> Pictorial form is the possibility that things are related to one another in the same way as the elements of the picture. (TLP 2.151)

Notice that in this last remark, Wittgenstein talks about the *possibility* of things being related in the same way as the elements of the picture. What this allows for is that the arrangement of marbles can both represent and also *misrepresent* how things are where I live: if I declare the first marble my house, the second marble the gas station, and the third Jimmy Snyder's house, then my arrangement shows how things *would be* if I lived closer to the gas station than to Jimmy Snyder. But so arranged, my marbles misrepresent where I live: so arranged, they say – or I say with them – something *false*.

In the arrangement of marbles, they are related to one another in a way that mirrors how the objects the marbles stand for are related – or can be related – to where I live. In relating them to one another, I do not need anything further – any further elements – to do so. I could, I suppose, add bits of string between each of the marbles, but that would not relate the marbles to one another so much as introduce new elements into the model that are related to the marbles and one another. My friend might ask, "What's with the bits of string?" and I could say that they stand for the road that runs past the two houses and the gas station. And here I do not need to add a further element for *running past*. If I start thinking of relations as further elements to add to the picture in order to relate the elements that stand for objects, I'm threatened with a regress of relations. That is why Wittgenstein says: "Instead of, 'The complex sign "aRb" says that a stands to b in the relation R', we ought to put, '*That* "a" stands to "b" in a certain relation says *that aRb*'" (TLP 3.1432).

There is another aspect of the arrangement of marbles that can be discerned without that involving the discernment or addition of any further objects or elements, no further marbles, bits of string, or anything like that. As seen in 2.15, Wittgenstein characterizes pictures or models in terms of *structure* and *form*, where the latter pertains to the possibility of the former. In my example, the marbles are arranged spatially to model how various places where I live are spatially related to one another. The form of the model is spatial in the sense that arranging and rearranging the spatial relations among the marbles changes what the model depicts. The *colors* of the marbles do not belong to the form, since nothing hangs on what color marbles I happened to choose. But in another kind of model, the color might play an important role (consider color-coded maps, for example) and in such models, colors are part of their structure and so color belongs to the form. The most basic notion of form – what binds together the different kinds of structures and their form (spatial, color-coded, etc.) – is *logical* form:

> A gramophone record, the musical idea, the written notes, and the sound-waves, all stand to one another in the same internal relation to depicting that holds between language and the world.
>
> They are all constructed according to a common logical pattern. (Like the two youths in the fairy-tale, their two horses, and their lilies. They are all in a certain sense one). (TLP 4.104)

I'll have more to say about the entirety of this passage shortly, but for now, I want to emphasize the middle sentence's appeal to a "logical pattern." Although my model consisting of an arrangement of just three marbles is pretty simple – it does not represent much about where I live beyond how a number of places are spatially related to one another – even so, it still has a kind of complexity. We can see this if we consider the question of just *what* it represents. Here are three things:

   i. Jimmy Snyder's house is south of my house
  ii. The gas station is south of Jimmy Snyder's house
 iii. The gas station is south of my house

So we can say that the model represents (i) *and* (ii) *and* (iii). The *and* is not a further object – a further representational element – in the model that I need to add (or could subtract). At 4.0311, Wittgenstein returns to the idea of things being combined so as to represent something: "One name stands of one thing, another for another thing, and they are combined with one another. In this way the whole group – like a *tableau vivant* – presents a state of affairs." Immediately following this remark – at 4.0312 – he writes:

> The possibility of propositions is based on the principle that objects have signs as their representatives.
>
> My fundamental idea is that the "logical constants" are not representatives; that there can be no representatives of the *logic* of facts.

Logic is not one more "ingredient" that I need to add to the model. Insofar as I have constructed a model at all with whatever pictorial form, it has a logical form. I cannot give the model a "different logic," as logic is not something I give to the model at all.

Consider again (i), (ii), and (iii). In addition to conjunction, we can see them as related via *implication*. What I mean here is that once we have (i) and (ii), then we also *already have* (iii). If Jimmy Snyder's house is south of my house and the gas station is south of Jimmy Snyder's house, then *it follows* that the gas station is south of my house. This is something we can *see* in the picture, in the way the marbles are arranged. I can make this more explicit perhaps by picking up and putting down the marble for Jimmy Snyder's house, as if to say "See, the gas station is also south of my house." Again, this can be seen in the picture without any further addition to the picture. I do not need to add further "representatives" to make it be that the marbles are so related. I do not, for example, need to add a *rule of inference* so as to make it be that (iii) follows from (i) and (ii), just as I do not need to add anything to my arrangement of marbles to give it logical form:

> If *p* follows from *q*, I can make an inference from *q* to *p*, deduce *p* from *q*.
> The nature of the inference can be gathered only from the two propositions.
> They themselves are the only possible justification of the inference.
> "Laws of inference," which are supposed to justify inferences, as in the works
>   of Frege and Russell, have no sense, and would be superfluous. (TLP 5.132)

I said just now that I cannot give the model a "different logic." I want to say more here about what that means. Consider a model where (i) and (ii) are represented, but where (iii) is not. Is there such a model? Can there be? How would I have to arrange my marbles so that Jimmy Snyder's house is south of my house and the gas station is south of Jimmy Snyder's house, but the gas station is not south of my house? I can rearrange the marbles so that one or both of Jimmy Snyder's house and the gas station are *north* of my house, but then that would not be a model where (i) or (ii) (or both) are represented. While I can misrepresent the arrangement of various buildings where I live,

I cannot misrepresent the logic of such arrangements (which is as much to say that I do not represent logic at all). At 3.031, Wittgenstein writes: "It used to be said that God could create anything except what would be contrary to the laws of logic. – The reason being that we could not *say* what an 'illogical' world would look like." While the emphasis here is on *saying*, the same holds for picturing or modeling. An "example" of an illogical world would be one where Jimmy Snyder's house is south of my house and the gas station is south of Jimmy Snyder's house, but the gas station is north of my house.[22]

That I used marbles to represent something about where I live is surely arbitrary. I could have used bits of paper, coffee cups, or even pieces of furniture as Wittgenstein suggests, just as I could have used dots on a piece of paper. I could even have sounded notes on a piano, with the note for my house being lower than the note for Jimmy Snyder's house, which in turn is lower than the note for the gas station (while the keys of the piano are separated spatially, their spatial arrangement would not belong to the form in the way the spatial arrangement belongs to the form of marble model). While there is this clear element of arbitrariness, once those arbitrary designations have been made – once I have designated which marbles stand for which buildings and once I have made clear that what matters is not their size or their color but how they are arranged on the coffee table – then there are things that are anything but arbitrary: "Although there is something arbitrary in our notations, *this* much is not arbitrary – that *when* we have determined one thing arbitrarily, something else is necessarily the case. (This derives from the *essence* of notation)" (TLP 3.342).

Although this last passage emphasizes notation, Wittgenstein's points about logical form and logical necessity do not pertain just to our ways of representing the world – to pictures and models – but to the world *represented*. After all, in 3.031's cashing out of the constraints on what God can and cannot create, he refers to an "illogical *world*." I said earlier that there was no model I could make – with my marbles or anything else – where Jimmy Snyder's house is south of my house, the gas station is south of Jimmy Snyder's house, but the gas station is north of my house. This is not a matter of an idiosyncratic inability on my part – the invocation of what God can and cannot do helps to emphasize this – nor is it an idiosyncratic feature of our resources for representing how

---

[22] I'm bracketing here the idea that we could on a globe arrive at the gas station (eventually!) by traveling *north*. That's not shown in the model I've constructed, but even if it were added in, it would also show that I could reach Jimmy Snyder's house in the same way *after* reaching the gas station and *before* reaching my house. I'm also assuming that it's understood that the structures – unlike the marbles – are stationary.

things are in the world. What pertains to the model pertains – and pertains *in the same way* – to the arrangement of the places being represented. Just as I cannot make a model where that inconsistent set of things holds, so too there cannot *be* an arrangement of houses and gas stations like that. Recall that pictures are themselves facts, just as how things stand with my house in relation to Jimmy Snyder's house and the gas station are facts. Hence, "logic pervades the world: the limits of the world are also its limits" (TLP 5.61).

1.2 From Solipsism to Realism

Wittgenstein's remark about logic pervading the world is immediately followed by 5.62, which begins by referring back to what has preceded it: "This remark provides the key to the problem, how much truth there is in solipsism." Given the numbering system of the *Tractatus*, "this remark" refers back to 5.6 rather than 5.61, as each are equally comments on 5.6 (were it referring to 5.61, its numbering should be 5.611). The remark in 5.6 reads: *"The limits of my language* mean the limits of my world." Just how *this* remark provides a key is far from clear. Before trying to make out how it might do so, we first need to get a sense for how the problem Wittgenstein refers to here even arises. How does solipsism come to be a problem or even come to look like an attractive option, especially in a work that so robustly appeals to the world and facts? We might start answering this last question by noting a feature of my example of building a model using marbles that suggests a problem in thinking it through. That is, there are limits to the model's efficacy as an example: probing those limits points toward a more general kind of problem or puzzle. Consider the question of how my little model comes to *be* such a model. We cannot in answering this question appeal to anything about the marbles themselves. As we noted previously, the choice of marbles was arbitrary beyond their having the right multiplicity and moveability. There's nothing *intrinsically* meaningful about marbles that makes them especially apt for – or immediately understood as – designating houses and gas stations. While three marbles lying on a table are by themselves caught up in a variety of facts – "There are three marbles on the table," "This marble is x inches away from that one," and so on – they do not *by themselves* represent anything at all. Taken by themselves, they are just marbles with their own properties, standing in various relations to one another (and to other things), but none of that *means*, *models*, or *pictures* anything.

What makes them a model depends upon *my making them* a model. I am the one who reaches for the marbles and endows them with significance, such that how they are arranged *stands for* how my house and other places around where I live are arranged. Without me – without what I *do* with the marbles – the marbles just are what they are and do not go proxy for anything. Although the arrangement of marbles can either get it right or get it wrong when it comes to representing how things are where I live, namely represent (or misrepresent) perfectly objective facts, their working that way relies on the workings of something *subjective*, a *subject* who imbues or endows the marbles and their arrangement with significance and so with the ability to depict something truly *or* falsely.

The question of how a model comes to be a model thus points in the direction of subjectivity, of a subject who makes what would otherwise just be – in this case – a bunch of marbles into a representation of something else. Let us consider further this idea of making something be meaningful, of endowing or imbuing something that by itself is meaningless with sense. In the case of the marbles, there appears to be a kind of easy answer to how such endowing or imbuing happens. The availability of such an easy answer reveals the limits of the marble example; probing those limits, however, helps to lead us in the direction Wittgenstein traces out in the *Tractatus* (and that he reports in the wartime notebooks) from idealism and solipsism to realism. First, the easy answer. When I first reached for the bag of marbles, I did so in response to a question asked by a friend about where I live. She did not ask the question using marbles, of course, but asked me in English. In response to her question, when I reached in the bag for some marbles, I too used English in order to designate what each marble stood for. I said things like, "Let's say this marble is my house" and "This marble is Jimmy Snyder's house" and so on. Had I instead silently laid out the marbles one after the other and then swept my hand across the array to draw my friend's attention to it, she would be more than a little puzzled as to what my little demonstration was supposed to show. She would not see how my array of marbles was meant to work *as* a model of anything. The words I speak as I pick out and arrange my marbles serve to *imbue* the marbles with meaning. I make them meaningful in part through what I say, in addition to how I lay them out on the coffee table. What this indicates is that the meaningfulness of the marbles is parasitic or derivative, as their meaning derives (at least in part) from the meaningful words that I speak as I construct my model. Wittgenstein writes at 4.021: "A proposition is a picture of reality: for if I understand a proposition, I know the situation it represents. And I understand the proposition without having had its sense explained to me." Since I *do* have to explain to my friend what I am up to with the marbles, the array of marbles is only a kind of ersatz proposition.

The problem we are after here is not just a problem about my particular example. I said before that the question about imbuing marbles with meaning admitted of an easy answer. What makes this answer *too* easy is that we are explaining the possibility of something's meaning something by appealing to something else that (already) means something: the meaningless marbles become meaningful because they get associated with an array of (already) meaningful words. We have answered one question – the question about how three marbles come to be a model – only to confront another one: how does what I *say* come to be meaningful? Just as, taken by themselves, marbles are only marbles, taken by themselves, the *sounds* I make or the *marks* I make on paper are just sounds and marks.[23] In other words, if there is nothing intrinsically meaningful about marbles, nothing that makes them naturally apt to designate things like houses and gas stations, then the same holds for sounds and marks: there is nothing *intrinsically* apt about the sequence of marks "house" for designating a house (one indication of this is that there are many other words in other languages that designate houses: *Haus, maison, casa, talo, nyumba*, and so on). It appears that they too must be imbued or endowed with meaning. If we avail ourselves of the easy answer again, then the problem is only pushed back another step. Whatever already meaningful signs I use to imbue the signs I used when imbuing the marbles with meaning will then need *their* coming to be imbued with meaning explained. And so on. Wittgenstein himself is acutely aware of this problem, as can be seen in the following passages from his wartime notebooks:

> How can I be *told how* the proposition represents? Or can this not be *said* to me at all? And if that is so can I "*know*" it? If it was supposed to be said to me, then this would have to be done by means of a proposition; but the proposition can only show it.

> What can be said can only be said by means of a proposition, and so nothing that is necessary for the understanding of *all* propositions can be said. (NB, 25)

So while I can explain to my friend what I'm up to with the marbles – the sense of the model *does* need to be explained – I do so using propositions whose shared meaning I take for granted. If I had to explain *those* as well, I would need yet another set of propositions whose shared meaning I take for granted. If those needed an explanation in turn, then we are in danger of an unstoppable regress.

The difficulty here is that we find ourselves wanting to explain how meaning is possible and yet whatever we appeal to, as already meaningful, only shifts the explanatory target one step further back. We seem to need a kind of "unexplained explainer," in the sense of something *intrinsically* meaningful that serves to endow everything else (signs, marbles, etc.) with meaning. In light of where we began this last series of reflections, it would appear that the source of this kind of intrinsic

---

[23] One indication of the persistence of this problem is PI, § 432: "Every sign *by itself* seems dead. *What* gives it life? In use it *lives*. Is it there that it has living breath within it? – Or is the *use* its breath?"

meaning must lie within the subject. Subjectivity is here understood as a kind of *power* whose exercise confers meaning on otherwise meaningless things, just as Midas had the power to turn things to gold with his touch. This way of thinking about subjectivity and its role in conferring meaning tends toward solipsism: since I do my own conferring – exercise my own power to imbue things with meaning – then those meanings through which the world makes sense belong to me alone. Hence the motivation to say: "The world is my world." If I alone do this kind of endowing, then I have no reason to think – no real way of knowing – that there is anything else that does any such conferring, let alone confer in the same way that I do.

We should not take these last ideas in stride, nor do I think Wittgenstein thinks we should. What is important is only seeing how we can feel pushed toward that way of thinking about meaning. There is something more than a little mysterious about this appeal to a kind of power inherent in subjectivity, as it is far from clear how it is meant to work. What does this subject – what do I – actually do to make something otherwise meaningless meaningful. Consider the inscription "house." How do I make that come to mean *house*? If I simply think to myself, "By 'house' I will hereafter mean *house*," the exercise seems empty on the face of it. The right-hand bit already uses "house" to mean *house*. There's also the problem of accounting for how I came to understand the scheme, "By X I will hereafter mean Y" (there are a whole lot of meaningful signs at work already!). Let's imagine that I'm standing in front of a house. I gaze intently at it while saying "house." What have I just done? Have I given the house a proper name, as though I had gazed at it and said, say, "Doug"? How would I show that I meant what I uttered in *that* way? Or have I named it in such a way that I can now talk about it *and other houses* using "house"? How is all of that contained in what happened when I directed my gaze house-ward and thought to myself, "house"? I need to know something more about what to *do* with "house," which means being able to use it in propositions, in pictures or models where it stands for or designates various houses: "In order to recognize a symbol by its sign we must observe how it is used with a sense" (TLP 3.326).[24] This last passage follows on from 3.3, where Wittgenstein says that "only propositions have sense; only in the nexus of a proposition does a name have meaning," and shortly thereafter, at 3.314, "An expression has meaning only in a proposition." Nothing in our imagined ritual with "house" reveals anything about how to use

---

[24] The sign-symbol distinction is crucial for understanding the *Tractatus*. At 3.32, Wittgenstein writes: "A sign is what can be perceived of a symbol" and then adds as commentary (3.321) that "one and the same sign ... can be common two different symbols – in which case they will signify in different ways." So we can think of the problem here as one of how signs come to symbolize *at all*.

"house" in a proposition, nor do we see how any ritual *like that* could instruct me on how to use it: "A sign does not determine a logical form unless it is taken together with its logico-syntactical employment" (TLP 3.327). I have to have a grip already on the idea of a proposition, which means that I already have to have a grip on some language or other.

This last point connects with the passage from the wartime notebooks cited earlier: "What can be said can only be said by means of a proposition, and so nothing that is necessary for the understanding of *all* propositions can be said" (NB, 25). Any explanation of how any particular signs come to have meaning will involve the use of further, already meaningful signs, whose coming to have meaning then needs to be explained. This in turn connects with what Wittgenstein says in the *Tractatus* about what the solipsist *means*: "For what the solipsist *means* is quite correct; only it cannot be *said*, but makes itself manifest" (TLP 6.62). One might be tempted to see in this remark only confusion, a "rung" on the ladder to be thrown fully away. My sense, however, is that there is a genuine insight here about the interplay between meaning and subjectivity: the very idea that one arrangement of things is a picture of anything else involves a subject *for whom* it is such a picture. This involvement is evident already in Wittgenstein's early talk of *making* pictures at 2.1 and his talk of *projection* in the early 3s. Where things go wrong – or become confused – is in thinking that we can make sense of this kind of making or projecting from the outside, from a place where, we might say, meaning has not happened yet. Such a place would afford us a glimpse of the workings of the "power" of subjectivity that endows otherwise meaningless elements into signs that symbolize. While we can see this power at work in *particular cases*, such as in my marble model, how it works there does not generalize. Solipsism goes wrong in thinking that it can. The attempt at generalization leads to thinking of this power as imbuing otherwise meaningless elements with meaning that *then* play a role in propositions, but without a grip on how propositions work – on how to make pictures – nothing can be picked out *as* a meaningful pictorial element.[25]

What we learn by thinking through the marble example to reveal its limits is not just something negative, namely, that the idea of subjectivity as a meaning-constituting power cannot be thought all the way through; we also gain a kind of positive insight regarding the *worldly* character of subjectivity. Being a subject

---

[25] That Wittgenstein is working here against the idea of there being something *added* to propositions so as to give them sense is central to Sullivan (1996); see especially 211–212. I have profited greatly from his discussion. See also Mounce (1997) for a careful exploration of the pitfalls of attributing to the early Wittgenstein a notion of intrinsically meaningful thought, which is "logically prior" to meaningful language. As Mounce notes: "I can speak of the world only because there is already a relation between the language I use and the world, only because there is an internal relation between the two" (7).

means having the ability to make pictures, which, as we have seen, are configurations of objects that represent other configurations of objects. That ability is itself a worldly ability and in two respects. Making pictures is a worldly *doing*: when I make a model for my friend to show her something about where I live, I avail myself of worldly items (the marbles) and explain what I'm up to using other worldly signs. In making a model, I am engaging in a world that my friend and I both encounter as meaningful: "the world is my world" insofar as I have the capacity to represent it, just as my friend has that capacity as well (otherwise there would be no point in arranging marbles for her). What models are – what we understand when we make them – are models *of the world*: "A proposition is a picture of reality: for if I understand a proposition, I know the situation it represents" (TLP 4.021). Even if I do not know whether what the proposition depicts really obtains – if what the proposition says is true – I still know something about the world, about what the world *would be* like if the proposition *is* true:

> In a proposition a situation is, as it were, constructed by way of experiment.
> Instead of, "This proposition has such and such a sense," we can simply say,
>   "This proposition represents such and such a situation." (TLP 4.031)

Understanding propositions – as representing the world – means understanding the world, how things are arranged in the world when a proposition is true and how things *could be* arranged even when a proposition is false. There is no sense of what a proposition is – what its sense is – apart from a sense of what it represents in the world.

Prior to these last remarks, back when Wittgenstein first introduces the idea of pictures and picturing, he characterizes pictorial form as "the possibility that things are related to one another in the same way as the elements of the picture" (TLP 2.151). This suggests that grasping that possibility is essential to understanding something – anything – as a picture. To understand a picture is to understand "how a picture is attached to reality," namely, by "reach[ing] right out to it" (TLP 2.1511). Wittgenstein goes on to talk about "the feelers of the picture's elements" by means of which "the picture touches reality." Even if I'm on the other side of the world when I construct my little marble model for my friend, it is nonetheless in contact with where I live as beholden to how things are where I live for its truth or falsity. If the marble model were not so beholden, then it would not *be* a model at all. It would be a model of something else or just a few marbles scattered on the coffee table. These early remarks can be brought to bear on the later discussion of solipsism, as they help to understand what Wittgenstein says both in the wartime notebooks and in the *Tractatus*. Here again are the relevant passages, starting with the notebooks:

> This is the way I have travelled: Idealism singles men out from the world as unique, solipsism singles me alone out, and at last I see that I too belong with the rest of the world, and so on the one side *nothing* is left over, and on the other side, *the world*. In this way idealism leads to realism if it is strictly thought out. (NB, 85)

> Here it can be seen that solipsism, when its implications are followed out strictly, coincides with pure realism. The self of solipsism shrinks to a point without extension, and there remains the reality co-ordinated with it. (TLP 5.64)

Wittgenstein's talk in the notebooks passage about belonging to the world accords with what I've been emphasizing about language as a worldly activity. The 4s of the *Tractatus* begin with the following: "A thought is a proposition with sense." Almost immediately – two remarks later – at 4.002, Wittgenstein connects the capacity to form and express thoughts through language to our embodied condition: "Everyday language is a part of the human organism and is no less complicated than it." I'll have more to say in subsequent sections about the appeal here to complexity, but for now I only want to call attention to the appeal to "the human organism," as it underscores the idea of belonging to the world that is represented in thought and language.

The self of solipsism "shrinks to a point without extension" insofar as the kind of power we've considered cannot be delineated without already involving what this power is alleged to create. As a self or subject, the would-be solipsist should be understood as having thoughts. In having the capacity to form thoughts, the solipsist has the capacity to make pictures. Pictures, as we have seen, are arrangements of elements that represent other arrangements of elements, *facts* that stand in a projective relationship to other *facts* so as to represent them. Rather than pulling the world within the purview of the solipsist's subjectivity, Wittgenstein's reflections on subjectivity's capacity to represent the world thrusts the subject out into the world. Hence the coincidence with "pure realism," as the capacity to represent is only operative in relation to a world to which the subject's thoughts "reach right out."

2 The Middle Wittgenstein

In this section, I consider Wittgenstein's stance toward realism and idealism in his writings of the early to mid-1930s.[26] These include works published as *Philosophical Remarks*, *Philosophical Grammar*, *The Big Typescript*, and *The Blue and Brown Books*. I will also draw on unpublished material from the

---

[26] See Stern (2018) for a good overview of Wittgenstein's work in the 1930s and its standing as a distinct period in his philosophical thinking and writing.

Nachlass. Of all of Wittgenstein's work, these writings contain the most references to realism and idealism. I will emphasize points of continuity with the *Tractatus*, while indicating significant points of departure as well. My sense is that those points of departure point the way in turn to ideas more fully worked out in the later writings, including the late writings beyond the *Philosophical Investigations*. Very roughly, the middle period preserves the world-involvement of thought and language that is central to the *Tractatus*, while moving away from the kind of *general* characterization of that involvement Wittgenstein tried to spell out in the early work. This flight from generality continues into the later period. Wittgenstein's growing emphasis on matters being *complicated* and *indeterminate* preclude the articulation of any kind of general thesis worthy of the name *realism* or *idealism*. While I am not in any way committed to seeing the work of the middle period as merely a prelude to the later work, I will be calling attention to ideas that emerge in the work of the 1930s that become more central as Wittgenstein's thinking evolves beyond the middle period.

2.1 Language and World

We saw from our examination of the *Tractatus* in the previous section that its vision of language is *world-involving* in at least three senses:

i.   As essentially representational, language is about the world
ii. As pictorial arrangements of elements, propositions are themselves facts (and the world is nothing other than "the totality of facts")
iii. Uttering propositions – making pictures or models – is an activity – something we *do* – within the world we represent with propositions. Signs symbolize in the use we make of them.

These three senses all contribute to Wittgenstein's handling of solipsism in the *Tractatus*. While rightly emphasizing that models are something made rather than found, the solipsist loses sight of the worldly character of those models. Although the solipsist may insist with some right, "These thoughts are mine," insofar as what belongs to the solipsist are *thoughts*, they are propositions that share a pictorial-logical form with what they purport to represent, namely, a worldly situation. Furthermore, nothing prevents other arrangements of elements from sharing that pictorial form with that worldly situation, and so there is nothing essentially "private" about the solipsist's thoughts. While right about *mineness* in some sense, the solipsist goes wrong in saying, "These thoughts are mine and *no one else's*." That is why "followed out strictly" solipsism "coincides with pure realism."

Despite the divergences we will later consider (Section 2.2), the middle writings continue to incorporate these three senses of world-involvement. Consider the following passage from *Philosophical Remarks*:

> Our expectation anticipates the event. In this sense, it makes a model of the event. But we can only make a model of a fact in *the* world we live in, i.e. the model must be essentially related to the world we live in and what's more, independently of whether it's true or false.
>
> If I say that the representation must treat of my world, then you cannot say "since otherwise I could not verify it," but "since otherwise it wouldn't even begin to make sense to me." (PR, § 34)

If I expect that it will rain this evening, then what I anticipate is a particular eventuality – rainfall in the evening – whose obtaining will count as the fulfillment of that expectation. When, come evening, I look out the window and see rain falling, I will understand what is happening as the fulfillment of what I expected: what I see out the window corresponds to the model of the situation at work in my expectation. In the same way, looking out the window in the evening and seeing only clear skies bears upon my expectation: I will thereby see that what actually happened did not match what I expected. All of this treats "of my world." Even in the case of more outlandish or farfetched models – that the rain this evening consists of neon green raindrops, for example – these are still models *of* the world: in understanding them, I understand what it would *be* for them to be true (even while being confident that nothing like that is really going to happen). In *The Big Typescript*, Wittgenstein reverts to talk of pictures, where understanding them means understanding *what* they represent, namely, something out in the world:

> If one means by a picture: the correct or false representation of reality, then one has to know of what reality or of what part of reality. I can represent this room correctly or incorrectly, but in order to find out whether my portrayal is correct or not, I have to know that it is this room that is meant. (BT, 226)

Understanding a picture – determining its accuracy or fidelity – is inseparable from understanding the world: I have to know what the picture is supposed to represent in order to gauge its fidelity to the world.

The middle period writings continue the *Tractatus'* vision of language at least inasmuch as it continues to reject what we might think of as a two-stage model of language wherein we can first make sense of having a language *and then* applying it to the world:

> Time and again the attempt is made to use language to limit the world and set it in relief – but it can't be done. The self-evidence of the world expresses itself in the very fact that language can and does only refer to it.

> For since language only derives the way in which it means from its
> meaning, from the world, no language is conceivable which does not repre-
> sent the world. (PR, § 47)

In keeping with the importance in the *Tractatus* of the sign-symbol distinction,
Wittgenstein continues to reject the idea that language consists of mere *signs*
that must be deciphered or interpreted to reveal an underlying thought: "If I give
someone an order then it is *quite enough* for me to give him signs. And I would
never say: These are mere words, and I have to get behind them" (BT, 4).
Wittgenstein continues within the same remark in *The Big Typescript* by noting
how signs symbolize in the same way across the first-person/third-person
divide: "But if someone says 'How am I supposed to know what he means,
all I see are his signs?', then I say: 'How is *he* supposed to know what he
means? – He too has only his signs'" (BT, 4). "Everything is carried out *in
language*," which means that "when I'm thinking in a language I don't have
additional meanings in mind running alongside the linguistic expression; rather,
language itself is the vehicle of thought" (BT, 283).

   In the *Tractatus*, signs symbolize in their use, what he refers to there as their
"logico-syntactical employment" (3.327). Similarly, in *Philosophical Remarks*, he
emphasizes how the *application* is "what makes the combination of sounds or
marks into a language at all" (PR, § 54). Wittgenstein here likens the use of
language to that of a measuring rod. Taken by itself, the rod is a mere stick with
marks on it, but "it is the application which makes the rod with marks on it into
a *measuring rod: putting* language *up against* reality" (PR, § 54). Here we can hear
an echo of the *Tractatus'* talk of a proposition's reaching "right out to" reality and
its being "laid against reality like a measure." The language we use to describe
reality and the reality described by language correspond or fit together in that we
use language to talk about both. When I expect that it will rain this evening, what
fulfills that expectation is nothing other than its raining in the evening: I pick out
the fact that fulfills my expectation using more or less the same words as I use to
articulate my expectation. Like "a convex shape fitting into a corresponding
concave shape ... the same description is valid for both" (BT, 266).[27]

2.2 Space and Spaces: Logic and Grammar

Wittgenstein develops the idea of "putting language up against reality" through
the idea of *space*, where he emphasizes the way meaning and the meant *share*
a space:

   The memory and the reality must be in *one* space.

   I could also say: the image and the reality are in *one* space. (PR, § 38)

---

[27] Wittgenstein concludes the remark with: "Compare a hat matching a dress."

In the case of the yardstick, this sense of a shared space is quite literal, as the measuring stick must be laid against whatever is being measured in order to determine its length. The measuring stick and what is measured share a space in that both are physical objects in a common physical space. In the *Philosophical Remarks*, Wittgenstein cautions against thinking of the physicality of the measuring stick as a liability, noting that "you cannot say: 'A ruler does measure in spite of its corporeality; of course a ruler which only has length would be the Ideal, you might say the *pure* ruler'." Determining the length of something involves using something that itself has length – a yardstick, measuring tape, and so on – that can be brought into contact with that object. The measuring and the measured can be compared only because they occupy the same space. Wittgenstein extends this sense of a shared space, albeit with some hesitancy:

"It's easy to understand that a ruler is and must be in the same space as the object measured by it. But in what sense are *words* in the same space as an object whose length is described in words, or, in the same space as a colour, etc.? It sounds absurd" (PR, § 46).

Although Wittgenstein here admits that "it sounds absurd," he nonetheless develops this idea of a shared space beyond the literal case of the measuring stick and the measured object. We can think of this more metaphorical sense of space as a *grammatical space*. Start with the yardstick: the yardstick has a grammar in the sense that it is constructed in a very specific way with a very specific way of being used. The yardstick is divided into uniform units (inches, feet) where the number of such units a measured object spans is the length of that object. To determine that length, one must know *how* to use the yardstick.[28] One must know, for example, that it must be laid against the object with the beginning of the yardstick at one end of the object (or one must know to subtract accordingly if only the middle of the yardstick is used). Someone who places the yardstick crosswise or perpendicularly to the object does not know how to use the yardstick properly, which suggests further that the person does not (yet) know what it means to *determine something's length*; the person does not (yet) know what length *is*. Knowing what length is involves knowing how to determine something's length, comparing the length of one thing to another, and so on, and all of that involves knowing how to "navigate" the space shared by things like yardsticks and measuring tapes, on the one hand, and the objects they can measure, on the other. Although we started this example by considering the physical or corporeal yardstick, which shares a literal space with the measured object, we can see that the sense of something being shared carries over to the *words* we use to talk about

---

[28] That our practices of measuring involve this kind of worldly know-how is a central theme of McManus (2012). My discussion here draws extensively on his examples and insights. See especially chapter 6, section 6.2.

the sizes of things: to be conversant in the language of measuring, where this means saying and understanding that something is some number of inches long, that one thing is longer than another, that two things are the same length, and so on, is inseparable from knowing how to use things like yardsticks. So while the yardstick literally shares the same space as the object measured by the yardstick – the yardstick is literally laid right up against the object to determine its length – the *language* of measuring shares that space as well in that the sense of that language is informed by the space of measuring.

Wittgenstein talks about other spaces in the middle-period writings, such as visual and auditory spaces, within which the languages of colors and sounds operate, as well as tactile space. Each of these spaces has a different grammar. Although we may use the same words in some cases – we talk of both *softer* and *louder* colors and sounds, for example – how these are determined and what they come to work differently in the two cases: a loud color does not occupy the same space as a loud sound. Understanding what colors and sounds are involves an understanding of their occupying these different spaces within which such determinations are made. "You cannot search wrongly; you *cannot* look for a visual impression with your sense of touch." This remark appears within a longer passage where Wittgenstein brings together talk of spaces, methods of searching, truth and falsity, and the image of the yardstick being laid against reality: "You cannot compare a picture with reality, unless you can set it against it as a yardstick" (PR, § 43).

The separateness of visual and tactile space rules out determining something's color with one's fingers. *Looking for a color* and *feeling for a texture* operate in different spaces that do not overlap. This lack of overlap informs Wittgenstein's use of "cannot" in the quote in the previous paragraph, which records a lack of *sense* rather than an inability. The *cannot* here is much like saying that one cannot score a touchdown in baseball: the "space" of baseball – its grammar – has no "place" for touchdowns, just as football has no place for double-plays and home runs.

In *The Big Typescript*, Wittgenstein continues this line of reasoning in differentiating between different kinds of misunderstandings:

> A misunderstanding is: "Is *this* an orange? I thought *that* was one."
>   What about this: "Is that *red*? I thought that was a *chair*."?
>   Can't one believe (if one doesn't understand English) that "red" means loud (is used as the word "loud" is actually is)? How would one clear up this misunderstanding? Something like this: "Red is this colour – not a volume." – Of course one could give such an explanation, but it would only be understandable to someone who already knows his way around in grammar. (BT, 31)

Note the difficulty Wittgenstein registers at the end regarding clearing up this kind of understanding. Saying to someone that red is a particular color rather than a volume will only help if that person has a general grip on colors and sounds, which means knowing "his way around in grammar."

Grammatical spaces are realms of *sense*, of different ways of making sense of the world. They are not detachable from the world, as they reflect different ways of navigating – and operating within – the world. "Grey must already be conceived as being in lighter/darker space if I want to talk of its being possible for it to get darker or lighter," to which Wittgenstein adds in the next line, "So you might perhaps also say: the yardstick must already be applied, I cannot apply it how I like; I can only pick out a point on it" (PR, § 42). We started this examination of Wittgenstein's appeal to meaning and the meant sharing a space as an extension of the *Tractatus'* talk of a proposition's reaching right out to the bit of reality it pictures. While there are clear lines of continuity, there are also significant points of departure. In the *Tractatus*, Wittgenstein talks about *the* space of sense – logical space – as what pervades both language and the world. In accordance with that kind of singularity, he also offers, at 6, the *general form of the proposition*. In *Philosophical Remarks* and beyond, a singular logical space is replaced by a plurality of grammatical *spaces*, different "chapters" of grammar that pervade or inform our talking about different domains of things: "The words 'Colour,' 'Sound,' 'Number' etc. could appear in the chapter headings of our grammar. They need not occur within the chapters but that is where their structure is given" (PR, § 2). This new emphasis on a *plurality* of grammatical spaces also means that the sense-nonsense distinction does not run along a single axis, such that nonsense could be ferreted out or avoided through a notation sensitive just to different logical types (first-order, second-order, and so on). Even variables on the same logical level would need to be further flagged or marked. "He listened to the whole sonata" and "He ate the whole banana" both make sense, whereas "He ate the whole sonata" and "He listened to the whole banana" do not, even though "banana" and "sonata" belong to the same (first-order) logical level. Anyone who knows anything about sonatas and bananas, and about eating and listening, can see that the latter pair does not make sense: like colors and sounds, bananas and sonatas are in different spaces.[29]

Indeed, accompanying this new talk of grammatical *spaces* are remarks explicitly on the *Tractatus* and its conception of generality. Although the idea of there being different "chapters" for grammar – in contrast to the unity of logic – appears from the outset of *Philosophical Remarks*, the consequences for

---

[29] However, in *Philosophical Grammar*, Wittgenstein writes: "When someone is taught language, does he learn at the same time what is sense and nonsense? When he uses language to what extent does he employ grammar, and in particular the distinction between sense and nonsense?" (PG, 190)

the idea of generality are drawn out more emphatically in *The Big Typescript*: "
If I ask 'What is the general form of a proposition?', then the counter-question
can be: 'Do we really *have* a general concept of a proposition, which we just
want to formulate exactly?' – Just like: Do we have a general concept of
reality?" (BT, 50)

Although Wittgenstein here answers his initial question only with a first and
then a second counter-question, he suggests a more definitive answer shortly
thereafter: "There are no such things as general discourses about the world and
language" (BT, 54). What's happening here?

Recall the passage I cited in the Introduction about Wittgenstein's interest
in language as a "spatial and temporal phenomenon" as emblematic of his
evolving stance on realism and idealism. In some ways, the roots of this idea
run all the way down to the *Tractatus*. Even there, Wittgenstein says that "all
the propositions of everyday language, just as they stand, are in perfect
logical order" (TLP 5.5563). Prior to that, he says at 4.002 that "everyday
language is part of the human organism and no less complicated than it."
This remark's appeal to the complexity of everyday language is coupled
with an idea of an underlying unity and simplicity.[30] In the latter part of the
passage, Wittgenstein likens the relation between language and thought to
that between clothing and the body, where language, like some kinds of
garments, *disguises* what lies underneath. This imagery points toward
a conception of *analysis* as geared toward revealing the true form.
Compare what he says about the *Tractatus* in *The Big Typescript*, shortly
after his questions concerning the general form of the proposition: "My view
in the *Tractatus Logico-Philosophicus* was wrong: 1. because I didn't
clearly understand the sense of the words 'a logical product is *hidden* in
a proposition' (and similar words), 2. because I too thought that logical
analysis would have to bring hidden things to light (as do chemical and
physical analysis)" (BT, 82).

As Wittgenstein moves through the middle period, he retains a sense of
everyday language as being complicated while jettisoning the idea of an
underlying simplicity, something hidden or disguised beneath the outer: "Is it
so to speak a pollution of sense that we express it in a particular language with
its contingencies, and not, as it were, disembodied and pure? No, for it's
essential that I understand the idea of translating from one language into
another" (BT, 177).

---

[30] See Cerbone (2019b) for extended discussion of this passage and its place in Wittgenstein's
evolving ideas on the contrast between *simple* and *complicated*.

Wittgenstein's linkage of translating one language into another to the rejection of a disembodied, "pure" conception of language retains and develops something else he says at 4.002 of the *Tractatus*. At the end of the remark, he notes that "the tacit conventions on which the understanding of everyday language depends are enormously complicated." Wittgenstein does not elaborate, but we might surmise here that such "conventions" concern different aspects of the way language is spoken (inflection, tone, cadence, and so on) as well as the bodily gestures and expressions that "accompany" what is said. Even without knowing a word of a foreign language, I can often gather something about what a person is saying in that language just by picking up on some of those things; as such, they give me a kind of foothold for working further to understand what that person is saying. As Wittgenstein's thinking evolves, he comes to recognize that these dimensions of speaking a language are not mere conventions or accompaniments, but integral to what language is and how language works: "Think of the multifariousness of what we call 'language'. Word-language, picture-language, gesture-language, sound-language" (PG, 179).

While in the *Tractatus* Wittgenstein says that "the world and life are one" (5.621), his writings in the middle period retain a sense of the significance of life – of language as woven into human life – while shedding the sense of unity found in the early work: "Well language does connect up with my own life. And what is called 'language' is something made up of heterogeneous elements and the way it meshes with life is infinitely various" (PG, 66).

2.3 Realism and Idealism Reconsidered

In this final section of our discussion of the middle period, I want to consider some of Wittgenstein's remarks explicitly on realism and idealism. *Philosophical Remarks* contains one of the earliest references to realism and idealism and pairs them as two sides of the same coin: " From the very outset 'Realism,' 'Idealism,' etc., are names which belong to metaphysics. That is, they indicate that their adherents believe they can say something specific about the essence of the world" (PR, § 55).

I cited this passage in the Introduction as exemplifying the neither-nor strand of Wittgenstein's attitude toward realism and idealism. That both "belong to metaphysics" and that both involve a belief in the ability to "say something specific about the essence of the world" do not indicate an approving stance. Wittgenstein's stance toward essences – especially the essence of the world – is mostly prohibitive in the *Philosophical Remarks*: "What belongs to the essence of the world cannot be expressed by language"

(PR, §54). The difficulty of such prohibitive remarks is that they seem to leave in place the idea that there *is* an essence of the world, but which cannot be expressed or captured in language. I think it is ultimately misleading to see Wittgenstein as here committed to an *inexpressible essence*. To see this, we have to consider what lies behind his use of *cannot* here. What makes language unsuitable appears to have to do with a shift in the use of words. That is, attempts to express the essence of the world use words that are ordinarily employed with a contrastive sense. Words such as *idea, appearance, the present*, and *existence* are not specialized or technical words: we often talk about our ideas or how things appear, appeal to what is happening in the present, and declare that something or other exists. But when we use words in these ways, we use them contrastively: ideas or appearances as opposed to things that are neither of those, what is happening in the present in contrast to the past or future, and something's existing rather than not (or no longer) existing. Statements of essence – as statements of how things *must* be – shed that contrastive or oppositional structure. If the would-be metaphysician declares that reality is essentially appearances or that only the present moment is real, then it is no longer clear what is being ruled out or excluded. However, if that is no longer clear, then it is not clear what to make of the initial claim to essence: if nothing can possibly be a *nonappearance*, then it no longer makes sense – or at least the same kind of sense – to designate something as *being* an appearance:

> If someone says, only the *present experience* has reality, then the word "present" must be redundant here, as the word "I" is in other contexts. For it cannot mean *present* as opposed to past and future. – Something else must be meant by the word, something that isn't *in* a space, but is itself a space. That is to say, not something bordering on something else (from which it could therefore be limited off). And so, something language cannot legitimately set in relief.
>
> The present we are talking about here is not the frame in the film reel that is in front of the project's lens at precisely this moment, as opposed to the frames before and after it, which have already been there or are yet to come: but the picture on the screen which would illegitimately be called present, since "present" would not be used here to distinguish it from past and future. And so it is a meaningless epithet. (PR, § 54)

Notice here Wittgenstein's appeal to the space within which talk of the present has its ordinary sense: that grammatical space is one where the present is contrasted with the past and the future. The "someone" he here imagines no longer means by "the present" something in that space; the present now "is itself a space."

Wittgenstein's reference to the word "I" connects this pair of paragraphs to the preceding pair, where he connects the difficulties involved in saying "only the *present experience* has reality" to *solipsism*: "The proposition that only the present experience has reality appears to contain the last consequence of solipsism. And in a sense that is so: only what it is able to say amounts to just as little as can be said by solipsism" (PR, § 54). This reference to solipsism is again followed by a more general prohibition on statements of essence: "For what belongs to the essence of the world simply *cannot* be said. And philosophy, if it were to say anything, would have to describe the essence of the world." However, he continues by giving philosophy a different task: "But the essence of language is a picture of the essence of the world; and philosophy as custodian of grammar can in fact grasp the essence of the world, only not in the propositions of language, but in rules for this language which exclude nonsensical combinations of signs" (PR, § 54).[31]

It is not entirely clear what Wittgenstein is after with his appeal to rules here, but what we noted earlier about contrastive senses and his example of the frame in the film reel give us some indication. Moreover, what we discussed earlier under the heading of *grammar* gives us a further sense of what Wittgenstein has in mind here. When we know our way about in grammar, we have a sense of what makes sense and what does not and this sense pertains both to language and what language is *about*: the grammar for talking about colors gives us a picture of the essence of colors; the grammar for talking about numbers gives us a picture of the essence of numbers; and so on. For example, it makes sense to talk about dividing a number into two other numbers, as when we divide eight into four and four, whereas it is not clear what it means to divide a *color* (at PG, 126, Wittgenstein considers the sense of "cutting red into bits"). We should not think of this grammar as *prohibiting* anything or as specifying anything we are *unable* to do, as though we, for example, cannot cut red into pieces while still allowing that something or someone else can. If anyone *does* talk sensibly of cutting red into pieces, then they are not talking about *red* in our sense of "red," that is, they are not talking about a *color*. These last reflections suggest that we should be careful not to read Wittgenstein's prohibitions on statements of essence as leaving the idea of the essence of the world firmly in place, while making a characterization of *it* somehow beyond our abilities. That

---

[31] This remark foreshadows PI, § 371: "*Essence* is expressed by grammar." This remark in turn is central to Anscombe (1981), which considers the question of linguistic idealism. While I will not be discussing this remark – or Anscombe's reflections – in the next section, it should be clear that "expressed by" should not be understood as identifying essence with grammar or asserting its dependence in a manner that invites the charge of idealism. See Ritter (2020): 29 for a rather brusque dismissal of Anscombe's concerns (with which I am not unsympathetic).

attempts at such characterizations result only in "meaningless epithets" undermines the idea of what we were trying to do.

Wittgenstein's remark in *Philosophical Remarks* about realism and idealism appears in close proximity to the remarks about the essence of the world just considered. They give us a sense of just how it is that idealism in particular misfires. Idealism presents itself as a kind of discovery concerning the nature of reality to the effect that reality consists of *appearances*, which are inherently bound up with minds. (Solipsism can here be seen as a natural consequence: if what is real is what is present to a mind, then what I know is real is only what appears to *my* mind; appearances that appear to other minds are nothing to me.) In keeping with this sense of discovery, idealism presents itself as *correcting* or *revising* how we think and talk about the world: whereas we initially took ourselves to be in touch with a variety of things "out there," all there (really) is are ideas, images, or appearances. So, to take an example from MS-178b – a short manuscript from this period[32] – the idealist proposes replacing statements such as "There is a chair in the room" with "A chair appears to me as being in this room" (or perhaps, "There seems to be a chair in the room"). The motivation for this suggested revision can be understood in two ways. The would-be idealist can provide an *epistemological* justification for the revision by casting it as a *safer* or more *cautious* manner of speaking: I can be sure of how things seem, while I may never know if there *really is* a chair there, as that would go beyond what it is possible for me to experience. Alternatively, the idealist can provide a kind of *ontological* justification by simply *identifying* the chair with (the sum of) appearances: the chair is *nothing more* than the various appearances we (or perhaps only I) experience.

Start with the epistemological version and the idea that it is *more cautious* to say only that there seems to be a chair rather than that there (really is) a chair. While the idea that it is a "safer bet" to say only that there appears to be a chair in the room seems to make sense, problems arise with this imagery of betting as we consider how, so to speak, the odds are calculated. If we say that it is safer to say there only seems to be a chair there *as opposed to* saying there (really is) a chair there, how do we determine degrees of risk in different cases? If, for example, there really being a chair there is construed as a hypothesis, in what way do various "seemings" contribute to confirming that hypothesis? What, we might ask, does the confirmation of the hypothesis look like? This last question suggests that we need to have at least some idea of what *there really being a chair there* involves, and so, correlatively, our *knowing there is really a chair*

---

[32] According to the Bergen archives, MS-178b dates from 1934, although that date appears with a question mark.

there, in order to understand and evaluate various cases where it seems that there is a chair. As Wittgenstein notes in MS-178b, if we replace "There is a chair there" with the idealist's preferred "The hypothesis that there is a chair here becomes more likely," the idea of a scale of likelihood is muddled, as we are treating our experiences as though they are approximations but without specifying the value to which they approximate:

> [How] did we arrange it? Always "There seems to be an armchair there" or also in one case: "There really is an armchair there"? Or does this expression not even exist in my language, but only this: "The hypothesis that there is a chair here becomes more likely." This would be like fx having no value for x = 0 but approximate values as we approach zero. But here the word "approximation" misleads as if these values are approaching a value & that's not the case, only x is approaching zero. So here the probability does not come close to a certainty, which is not unreachable owing to human weakness. Rather, we have provided no such certainty (like no such value f(0)) in our game. (BNE, MS-178b, 1[3]-2[1])

Without a sense of what it means to say that there really is a chair there – of what it means to know that there is a chair there – the idea of restricting oneself to – or *settling for* – appearances out of a sense of epistemological caution is undermined. The usual sense of "There seems ... " is tied to the sense of "There (really) is ... ": we say both that things only seem a certain way, but actually are not, and also that things sometimes are as they seem. Talk of seeming is part of the same game as talk of being. The epistemologically motivated idealist relies upon that contrast to give the proposed theory the air of a discovery, but what initially presents itself as a kind of theoretical insight turns out to be another way of talking whose sense has not been made clear:

> Someone who says we can actually never know whether there really is a chair here determines a grammatical game. (And establishes no fact about our human capacity.)
> We could ask him: "What do you even call 'knowing that there is a chair'"? (BNE, MS-178b, 2[3])

As Wittgenstein says in the sequel: "And we can hold up our normal language to him & say 'but I know there's a chair here'. And this mode of expression is no less precise than his" (BNE, MS-178b, 3[1]).

The difficulties facing the more epistemologically minded idealist might seem to be diminished by transposing the doctrine into a more ontological register. So transposed, idealism no longer has to have a metric for determining the "safety" of different "bets," as there is no longer a *real chair* apart from – or over and above – chair-appearances. However, the gains of transposing the idealist position into a more ontological register are illusory, as the new position inherits the problems of the old one. If this second form of idealist says that the chair – what we mean by "chair" – is nothing more than the sum of chair-appearances, we are again jettisoning the contrastive case that animates talk of appearances in the first place: what are *appearances* if everything is? In order to be a substantive theory – or be making a substantive claim – the idealist must be ruling something out. What there is must be appearances *rather than* something else, but this is what the "theory" effectively denies. The idealist is again offering a new grammatical game, where talk about things like chairs is replaced with talk about appearances of chairs. What is new about the grammar of the idealist's game is that "appearances" in the new game does not have the same valence as before, as its meaning does not involve a contrast between appearing and being. If being just is appearing, then appearing does not mean what it meant in the game we had been playing up until the idealist's discovery. Of course, the idealist is free to play whatever game she/he likes. Where the idealist goes wrong is in thinking that the new game bears upon the old game either by encouraging us to be epistemologically more responsible or by more accurately determining the essence of the world.

The passages I have cited from MS-178b precede a remark that provides a kind of summary of how Wittgenstein sees the interplay between realism and idealism. Although I have been stressing his dissatisfaction with idealism's attempt to "say something about the essence of the world," his endorsement of realism is not without qualification either:

> Realism says that what we say in ordinary language is correctly expressed. Idealism claims that it was expressed essentially incorrectly & one should actually say it differently. Roughly speaking, we must first say that realism is right, but then we must stop the nonsense of the [realist's] conception of language, which is the real reason for the idealistic objections. (BNE, MS-178b, 6[1])

Saying that (roughly) realism is right accords with the confusions that beset idealism's corrective impulses: what the idealist presents as a discovery that motivates a revision of our usual ways of thinking and talking is instead a proposal for a new way of talking whose sense has not yet been determined. Idealism goes wrong in pretending that it can retain the senses bound up with our usual ways of thinking and talking, while rejecting key aspects of what animates those senses in the first place. Notice, though, that Wittgenstein does not stop with this nod toward realism; instead, he expresses some sympathy for idealism as well. The sympathy expressed here is akin to another remark in a different manuscript from roughly the same period:[33] "Realism is always right

---

[33] As noted earlier in footnote 32, MS-178b dates from 1934, although that date appears with a question mark, while MS-156b is dated 1933?–1934.

in what it says. But idealism sees problems that are there and that realism does not see" (BNE, MS-156b, 22 v).

It is not clear whether the problems Wittgenstein refers to in this last remark have to do with the realist's nonsense (*Unfug*) conception of language in the MS-178b passage. In any event, neither remark is particularly forthcoming about what sorts of problems are at issue or what sort of nonsense is involved in a realist's conception of language. Indeed, it is not clear just what that conception is.

Two remarks after his characterization of realism and idealism in MS-178b, Wittgenstein returns to the contrast between the appearing of an object and the object itself:

> An infinitely strange (*seltsam*) problem (or disquietude [*Beunruhigung*])[34] arises in us when we look at any spatial object when we try to become conscious of what this body is actually like, since we only have one side and therefore in a certain sense do not see it. (7 [1])

The problem or disquietude Wittgenstein describes here might be understood as a kind of point of origin for both realism and idealism, as it concerns an anxiety about our "access" to the object, to what the object is "actually like." The trajectory of the remainder of the passage tends back toward idealism's attempt to quell this anxiety by equating the object with the semblance of the object, which Wittgenstein here sees as mistakenly treating a grammatical connection between appearing and being (where appearances are, after all, the appearances *of* something) as a result of *analysis*: the object *is* the appearances in the way that water *is* a compound of hydrogen and oxygen. The realist, by contrast, recoils from this disquietude in the opposite direction: whereas the idealist assimilates what appears to its appearings, the realist severs the connection entirely, thereby conceiving of what there is potentially having nothing in common with the way things appear to us. In a passage that appears in both *Philosophical Remarks* and *The Big Typescript*, Wittgenstein complains of an attitude wherein "this which we take as a matter of course, *life*, is supposed to be something accidental, subordinate: while something that normally never comes into my head, reality!" (PR, § 47; BT, 315). Such an attitude attempts to conceive of the "essence of the world" apart from anything that "comes into my head," in other words, apart from any conception of the world drawn from how the world appears. What resources the realist can marshal in this attempt is far from clear, as they could not include anything pertaining to appearances. As with the idealist, the realist illustrates the way an attempt to characterize the

---

[34] Consider also PI, § 111 which talks about "deep disquietudes (*tiefe Beunruhingen*)" arising from "a misinterpretation of our forms of language."

"essence of the world" neglects the grammatical space within which words have their sense.

While something like this criticism appears to be in play in Wittgenstein's attitude toward realism, which explains his often treating realism and idealism as two sides of one metaphysical coin, it does not really mesh with the complaint about the realist's *Unfug* conception of *language* that supposedly gives the idealist leverage in the first place. His talk in the passage from *Philosophical Remarks* and *The Big Typescript* about treating *life* as "accidental" and "subordinate" perhaps provides a clue, as it suggests that the realist neglects the way language and life are woven together. Recall how in the *Tractatus* there was a kind of pull toward subjectivity in the idea that we *make* models of reality. Wittgenstein's appeal here to *life* echoes that kind of pull: the life of language is not something apart from our lives. As he also says in MS-178b, immediately prior to the remark where he mentions the realist's problematic conception of language, "language is the phenomenon of people speaking with one another" (BNE, MS-178b, 5[1]). There is something in this seemingly unobjectionable remark that bothers the realist: that these grammatical spaces are spaces *we* navigate – that we sustain by using them to talk about all the things we talk about – somehow compromises them when it comes to talking about the world. A truly objective language would be a language uncompromised by our speaking it, a language that articulates the world but no one speaks. The idealist rightly recoils from this idea, which is, after all, just one more of *our* ideas, but goes wrong in assimilating the world to the language(s) we use to articulate it. Both thus misunderstand the ways in which language "meshes with life." That these ways are "infinitely various" is a theme that only becomes more prominent as we move into the later period.

3 The Later Wittgenstein

References to realism and idealism fall off dramatically after the early to mid-1930s. While draft versions of the Preface to the *Philosophical Investigations* in MS-117 include the "opposition between realism and idealism" in the list of topics to be treated in the work, that subject is dropped from later, more polished versions. At most, realism and idealism are relegated to the "other things" that conclude the list of topics Wittgenstein cites in the opening paragraph. And indeed, neither "realism" nor "idealism" appears anywhere in the *Investigations*. There is instead only one reference to the *realist* and the *idealist*, which I cited in the Introduction. These two figures appear in other later manuscripts as well: the second volume of *Remarks on the Philosophy of Psychology* contains a series of remarks on the realist and the idealist that is reproduced in *Zettel*, and remarks in a similar vein can also be found in *On Certainty*.[35] As with the passage in the *Investigations*, Wittgenstein's primary concern is to determine just what kind of *dispute* there is between the realist and idealist: what are they disagreeing about and how does that disagreement make any kind of difference in what they say and do? As Wittgenstein notes midway through the series, "But the idealist will teach his children the word 'chair' after all, for of course he wants to teach them to do this or that, e.g. to fetch a chair. Then where will be the difference between what the idealist-educated children say and the realist ones?" (RPP II, § 339/Z, § 414). This concern is not at all foreign to the material we examined in the previous section; instead, it might be understood as representing further reflection on those extended discussions in the typescripts and manuscripts of the 1930s. There, Wittgenstein had challenged the idea that idealism has made any kind of *discovery* about either the nature of reality or our "access" to it via its appeal to *appearances*. In the later remarks, Wittgenstein questions the sense of that discovery by asking us to consider how words for things are learned and where the appeal to appearances might figure into that process. Just like the would-be realist, the idealist will teach his children the word "chair" *first*, and this will be done in part by teaching the children to fetch chairs, arrange and rearrange them, and so on. Only afterward might the idealist introduce talk of chair-appearances and the like, which again underscores the way talk of appearances is interwoven with talk of the things that appear. The sense of discovery is further undermined by noting how what the children *do* with chairs will be unaffected by any later instruction about appearances: the idealist's children will carry on with chairs just as before. But if there is something problematic about the *sense* of the idealist's discovery, then there is something equally odd about the realist's attempt to counter it. If the realist simply reiterates the kinds of things we already say, then she has not yet put forward any kind of view or theory. If, however, the realist intends to offer a *thesis* that insists on the reality of things beyond *appearances*, then the realist betrays a reliance on the idealist's claimed discovery whose sense has not been made clear.

Notice Wittgenstein's challenging the genuineness of the dispute between realism and idealism via a question concerning the *teaching* and *learning* of language. To use Wittgenstein's example, for both the realist and idealist, their children's learning to talk about chairs is bound up with their learning to sit on chairs, fetch them, count them, rearrange them, and so on. As Wittgenstein notes about the children when it comes to chairs and the like: "There isn't any question of certainty or uncertainty yet in their language-game. Remember:

---

[35] See RPP II, §§ 338–341 (Z, §§ 413–416). See also OC, §§ 19, 24, and 37.

they are learning to *do* something" (RPP II, § 341/Z § 416). That we learn to speak – learn a language – is of paramount importance in the *Philosophical Investigations* and elsewhere in Wittgenstein's later writings. Being reminded of this obvious fact – that language is taught and learned – reminds us that both the learning and the speaking of language happen within a broader setting, our ongoing lives in the world and with one another. Wittgenstein's interest in the *natural setting* of language learning and use serves to continue the trajectory we followed in the previous section. The flight from generality and the emerging emphasis on the variety and indeterminacy of language tell against the articulation of a general thesis along the lines of either realism or idealism, as there is no clean sorting of things into the kinds of categories necessary to formulate either of the two positions. I will try in this section to spell this out in more detail via attention to the *Philosophical Investigations* and other writings from the later period, including the various manuscripts on the philosophy of psychology. In doing so, I will also address readings of Wittgenstein that see in his later work a commitment to some kind of idealism despite the relative paucity of references to both realism and idealism. I will consider his very last writings – published as *On Certainty* – separately.

3.1 Against Essence: Variety and Indeterminacy

Two of the themes that I want to emphasize appear throughout the later writings: the open-ended variety of language and the idea of language as a natural historical phenomenon. One measure of their importance is their presence from the very beginning of the *Philosophical Investigations*, where Wittgenstein offers his first "sketches" of key ideas that recur throughout the subsequent remarks as they "criss-cross ... over a wide field of thought" (PI, Preface). These are not at all separate ideas for Wittgenstein but feed into one another: that language is bound up with ongoing human activity – our *form of life*[36] and its natural history – accounts for its variety and indeterminacy. Human life, although informed by relatively stable and recurring patterns underwritten by a variety of organic constants, is not fixed and static; insofar as the use of language is integral to human life, it is neither fixed nor static either. As he says in one of the later manuscripts: "If a pattern of life is the basis for the use of a word then it must contain some amount of indefiniteness. The pattern of life, after all, is not one of exact regularity" (LW I, § 211). As this remark illustrates, our two key ideas are hardly confined to the *Investigations*. We can begin, however, by noting the appearance of these themes and their interrelation in the

---

[36] See Boncompagni (2015) and Boncompagni (2022) for further discussion of the idea of *forms of life* in Wittgenstein's later philosophy.

opening sections of the *Investigations* before attending to their treatment in other later manuscripts.

By the opening sections of the *Investigations*, I mean §§ 1–36, which I read as setting a kind of agenda for the text more broadly; after these opening remarks, Wittgenstein begins to zero in on particular topics, such as the name-bearer relation, understanding and explanation, the nature of philosophy, rule-following, and so on. The *Investigations* begins famously with a passage from Saint Augustine, wherein he recounts his entry into language by attending to his elders' use of words in conjunction with their pointing and moving toward various items in their shared environment. Although Wittgenstein's commentary begins with his adducing a "picture of the essence of language"[37] whose criticism will shape and inform the unfolding discussion, we should not take the passage from Augustine as serving only as critical fodder. That is, the quoted passage announces positive themes[38] as well insofar as it highlights the idea of language as something *shared* and *learned*, and as woven together with such things as *gestures* – what Augustine refers to as "the natural language of all peoples"[39] – along with *facial expressions*, the *movement of the limbs* and *the tone of voice*, which in turn are connected to both positive and negative *desires*. The child's attunement to these dimensions of his elders' activities – his natural tendency to absorb and emulate these patterns of activity – is integral to his entry into language. Wittgenstein's deployment of the builders starting in § 2 again connects the use of language to a broader activity – in this case, an assistant's fetching various building materials in response to a builder's words – even while suggesting the poverty of the idea that the meaning of "every word" in a language is "the object for which the word stands" (PI, § 1). Wittgenstein's use of the builders illustrates his method of *language-games*. Imagining simple, primitive games like that of the builders "disperses the fog" that "surrounds the working of language" (PI, § 5). However, this sense of *language-game* is only one of several, as § 7 makes clear. After first recalling "the practice of language (2)," with its simple pattern of calling out words

---

[37] Wittgenstein first spells out this picture in PI, § 1 as consisting of three ideas: "Every word has a meaning. This meaning is correlated with the word. It is the object for which the word stands." Given the positive dimensions of the passage from Augustine, to see in this passage such a picture is already to be in its grip. See Cavell (1995) and Goldfarb (1983) for discussions of the richness and density of these opening remarks.

[38] The closing paragraphs of the second lecture of Cavell (1990) provides an inventory of Augustine's "scene of instruction," which, in Cavell's words, "haunts the *Investigations* as a whole" (98).

[39] Something very close to this idea is offered in Wittgenstein's own voice at PI, § 206: "Shared human behaviour is the system of reference by means of which we interpret an unknown language."

while another "acts on them" and adding further simple patterns such as a language learner naming objects or, "even simpler," a learner repeating the words after the teacher, Wittgenstein then writes in the three further paragraphs the remark comprises:

> We can think of the whole process of using words in (2) as one of those games by means of which children learn their native language. I will call these games "*language-games*" and sometimes speak of a primitive language as a language-game.
>
> And the processes of naming the stones and repeating the words after someone might also be called language-games. Think of certain uses that are made of words in games like ring-a-ring-a-roses.
>
> I shall also call the whole, consisting of language and the activities into which it is woven, a "language-game." (PI, § 7)

The last sense of "language-game" in this passage is the one I want to highlight, as it calls attention to the ways that speaking a language is bound up with – or woven into – a broader range of activities. This last sense of "language-game" foreshadows what Wittgenstein says at § 19: "And to imagine a language means to imagine a form of life."

The import of this last idea is (at least) twofold: first, that language is bound up with forms of life – customs, practices, activities – suggests already that language is a variegated and diverse phenomenon. Just as there is a wide variety of customs, practices, and activities across different times and places, so too is there a variety of "language-games" that we should not expect to work in the same way across the board (in contrast, for example, to a reductive word-object relation). This idea appears in the first remark of the *Investigations*, where the example of the shopkeeper elicits the question of the meaning of the word "five" (in contrast to a word like "apple"); it is then treated more explicitly shortly thereafter via Wittgenstein's analogy between the words of a language and tools in a toolbox. Just as the latter have a variety of uses and do not work in uniform ways, so too should we not expect words to be comprehensible in terms of a uniform function: "Think of the tools in a toolbox: there is a hammer, pliers, a saw, a screwdriver, a rule, a glue pot, nails and screws. – The functions of words are as diverse as the functions of these objects. (And in both cases there are similarities)" (PI, § 11).

To turn to the second point of importance, that language is bound up with forms of life that are *ongoing* and *changing* tells against the idea that we can think of the phenomenon of language as *bounded* and *complete*. This latter idea is the topic of § 18, which immediately precedes the invocation of a form of life. There, Wittgenstein invites us to think of "our language" on analogy with an "ancient city" that has grown and changed over time:

Don't let it bother you that languages (2) and (8) consist only of orders. If you want to say that they are therefore incomplete, ask yourself whether our own language is complete – whether it was so before the symbolism of chemistry and the notation of the infinitesimal calculus were incorporated in to it; for these are, so to speak, suburbs of our language. (And how may houses or streets does it take before a town begins to be a town?) Our language can be regarded as an ancient city: a maze of little streets and squares, of old and new houses, of houses with extensions from various periods, and all this surrounded by a multitude of new suburbs with straight and regular streets and uniform houses. (PI, § 18)

Notice how the organic imagery Wittgenstein uses here to underscore the living and evolving dimensions of language incorporates the idea of diversity we initially considered: the "ancient city" he pictures here is marked by a wide variety of structures and spaces that are organized in markedly different ways. Notice too the absence of cut-off points at both ends: just as Wittgenstein's parenthetical question does not admit of a decisive answer (such as "More than ten houses and at least two streets that cross one another"), there is no point at which one can say about a language, "There now – it's complete. We'll never need another word or expression or way of saying anything."

In the 20s of the *Investigations*, Wittgenstein underscores the importance of the final sense of "language-game" he offered back at § 7: "The word 'language-*game*' is used here to emphasize the fact that the *speaking* of language is part of an activity, or form of life" (PI, § 23). This appears in the middle of a long remark, which Wittgenstein begins by asking, "But how many kinds of sentences are there?" to which he responds, "There are *countless* kinds; countless different kinds of use of all the things we call 'signs,' 'words,' 'sentences.'" To illustrate, Wittgenstein provides a fifteen-line list of things we do with words – telling a story, making up a joke, describing the results of an experiment, solving a math problem, and so on – whose deliberately motley character resists further systematization or regimentation. The list could (obviously) be continued and there seems to be little point in numbering the first item on the list with a "one" in the hopes of numbering a *final* entry (indeed, the final line of the list includes "requesting, thanking, cursing, greeting, praying" and so hardly counts as a single entry). The passage concludes with a backward glance at Wittgenstein's own earlier philosophical thinking: "– It is interesting to compare the diversity of the tools of language and of the ways they are used, the diversity of kinds of word and sentence, with what logicians have said about the structure of language. (This includes the author of the *Tractatus Logico-Philosophicus*.)" (PI, § 23).

Recall from the discussion of Section 1 the single-minded ambition of the *Tractatus* to limn the structure of the proposition in order to display its capacity for representing facts. What Wittgenstein refers to in the *Tractatus* as *logical form* is conceived there as what is essential to propositions; moreover, logical form is conceived of as singular – *the* logical form – and fully general: proposition 6, which offers "the general form of the proposition," is a climax of sorts for the work (where the silence invoked in the closing proposition serves as a dénouement). While some of the items on Wittgenstein's motley list of § 23 could be accommodated by the *Tractatus*, many of the others have no place in the economy of that work; they simply do not register as being of interest or importance.

These opening passages signal a continuation of what I referred to in the previous section as a flight from generality. Nothing in the later developments of the *Investigations* does anything to halt that flight: at § 65, for example, Wittgenstein explicitly raises the question of the *essence* of language only to turn it aside by introducing the idea of *family resemblances*. Equally important is the way this vision of language as involving open-ended variety is woven together with an emphasis on language as part of our *natural history*: "Giving orders, asking questions, telling stories, having a chat, are as much a part of our natural history as walking, eating, drinking, playing" (PI, § 25). Wittgenstein's appeal here to our natural history helps to underwrite and make sense of the kind of diversity of language – of kinds of sentences – that figures in these opening remarks. Our natural history, while marked by common elements that reach down to include basic biological functions, is nonetheless marked by diversity and variety. Our human form of life includes many different forms, different ways of living and making a living: different customs, practices, rituals, social orders, styles of dress, modes of building, and so on. Moreover, our natural history is not something finished but continues into an indefinitely longer or shorter future, and so will no doubt involve further variety and diversity.

3.2 The Natural and the Magical

I want to point to one further idea in the opening passages of the *Investigations* that follows on from what we have discussed earlier. This further idea also marks a point of continuity with the *Tractatus*, despite the critical tone of Wittgenstein's reference to it at § 23. In offering the final sense of "language-game" in § 7 – the sense I have been emphasizing throughout – Wittgenstein specifies that the term refers to a *whole* that includes both the "language and the activities into which it is woven." Although a very early passage, it is already the second time that Wittgenstein invokes the idea of a *whole*. He concludes the lengthy § 6, which concerns how instruction might effect a "connection" between a word and a thing, by noting: "'I set the brake up by connecting the rod and lever.' – Yes, given *the whole* of the rest of the mechanism. Only in conjunction with that is it a brake-lever, and separated from its support it is not even a lever; it may be anything, or nothing" (PI, § 6 – my emphasis).

The closing "It may be anything, or nothing" indicates the importance of "the whole of the rest of the mechanism." Without that "whole" the rod and lever would not *be* a brake; only so connected do those parts have that function. Those very same items – the rod and lever – could be something entirely different – have an entirely different function – if integrated into a different mechanism. The importance of being integrated into a broader whole carries over into the subsequent section's introduction of language-games as an interweave of language and activities. Notice further how Wittgenstein's motley list of § 23, offered to motivate the idea that there are "countless" kinds of sentences, is a list of activities, of our *doing* things that involve doing things with language. As with the brake-lever, we might say that *only in conjunction* with these activities are the words and gestures what they are. They have meaning within these surroundings, connected to the rest of "the mechanism."

Drawing our attention to the importance of "the whole" – of the inter-weave of language and activities – helps to motivate the third idea, which Wittgenstein begins to lay out toward the end of the opening remarks. We can think of this third idea as involving a rejection of a kind of *isolationist* conception of meaning; we can also think of it as involving a rejection of a *magical* conception of how language works (or of exposing a conception of how language works *as* magical). The first inklings of this idea emerge as early as § 6's discussion of an "associative connection" between word and thing – "Uttering a word is like striking a note on the keyboard of the imagination" – but it gains prominence in the discussion of pointing and ostensive definition in the late 20s. What the latter discussion emphasizes is the way the gesture of pointing *taken by itself* does not suffice to define a word. The "grammar" of the word whose meaning I'm emphasizing by my gesture must already be in place for the gesture to have a point. We can, when we point, point to all manner of things: something's shape, color, texture, number, even price ("Now that's an expensive vase!"). Wittgenstein is not casting doubt on our ability to do so – it would be absurd to say that I cannot point to a thing's color or that no one can ever really know if I am pointing to something's color rather than its shape – but he wants us to notice how that ability is not something freestanding. *If* all we had was the gesture plus some vocable, *then* what we are doing by pointing and uttering that vocable would not be enough to determine – let alone instruct someone on – the meaning of the word.

At this juncture, the following thought proves tempting. *Of course*, the gesture and the vocable do not suffice, but something crucial has been left out: when I point and say "Blue" (or "Two" or "Triangle" or . . .) I also *think* about what I want to point to; my thinking of the color (rather than the number, shape, or what have you) is what *fixes* or *determines* my gesture. Here we are in the vicinity of a magical way of thinking, as we are appealing to the mind as having a special kind of power to make things meaningful. Before considering Wittgenstein's response in these early remarks of the *Investigations*, it should be noted that we have encountered this temptation before. In spelling out the allure of solipsism, I noted the pull toward thinking of the mind – or of thought – as being the source that endows or imbues models with meaning, as what makes arrangements of things into models that represent (possible) facts. However, we also saw how any attempt to catch that special power in action always comes too late, so to speak, as its operation always already involves the use of meaningful signs. Despite Wittgenstein's criticisms of his earlier work in the vicinity of these remarks, I think we can see this latest trajectory of his thinking as a continuation of his earlier ideas.

Let's consider more closely how this appeal to the mind is supposed to work here. I point to something blue and say "Blue." As I do so, a blue patch appears in my mind (it sounds, so to speak, on the keyboard of my imagination). What has that third thing – the appearing of the patch before my mind – added? In what way is it the missing ingredient? Rather than a missing ingredient, the addition of a "mental patch" only compounds the problem, as we can now ask what it is about the appearance of this patch in my mind that makes it an occurrence of a thought about *color*. How is it that I am thinking about the color of the patch rather than its shape or texture or time of appearance or . . . ? If I must, in the case of the patch, do something to note its color rather than anything else, then the appeal to the patch seems to be an extra shuffle, as we might well wonder why I didn't just do that in order to note the color of the original thing. The redundancy can be made more evident if we follow the kind of advice Wittgenstein offers in the *Blue Book*[40] when it comes to the temptation to appeal to the presence of something to or in the mind that does some special work: instead of a patch appearing in my mind, imagine instead that I have a blue piece of paper in my pocket or even a color chart. I point to the object whose color I am trying to indicate and then pull out the piece of paper and point to that. But how am I pointing to the color in the latter case in some special way?

---

[40] Wittgenstein offers this advice at BBB, 4. The papers collected in Stroud (2002) attest to its importance.

I could again be pointing to the shape of the piece of paper or its being made of paper or what have you. Of course, if I know my colors (and if you know yours), then noting the color of either the object in question or the imagined patch, rather than, say, its shape, is generally not a problem. Again, we do such things *all the time*, but we can do so because we are already familiar – or conversant – with colors, which means that no special mental power is operative *in that moment alone* to fix what I point to.

Wittgenstein lays out these ideas at §§ 29–35 of the *Investigations*, which begins with the following:

> Perhaps someone will say, "two" can be ostensively defined only in *this* way: "This *number* is called 'two'." For the word "number" here shows what *place* in language, in grammar, we assign to the word. But this means that the word "number" must be explained before that ostensive definition can be understood.

Wittgenstein develops this initial point in a way that deflects the kind of magical thinking we sometimes find tempting: "Whether the word 'number' is necessary in an ostensive definition of 'two' depends on whether without this word the other person takes the definition otherwise than I wish. And that will depend on the circumstances under which it is given, and on the person I give it to" (PI, § 29).

Saying that "it depends" suggests that there is no one thing that must occur either in conjunction with my gesture or on the part of the audience in order to secure the meaning of the gesture. This is not to say that the gesture *cannot* be secured, but only that how it is depends. If I'm teaching number words to a child, I will likely do something different than if I'm reviewing number words with a native speaker of another language who is learning English. In the latter case, I can revert to the speaker's home language – if I know enough of it – to make clear that "two" is a number word, but there is no such option in the case of a child (as Wittgenstein notes at §32, we should not think of the child's entry into language as a matter of coming into "a foreign country" and not understanding "the language of the country; that is, as if he already had a language, only not this one"). Children do, of course, learn number words, words for colors, and so on, and how they do so is a complicated process that involves picking up both the vocabulary *and* the grammar: children learn these things by *doing* lots of things, such as sorting, counting, building, coloring, and they do so within a broader array of activities such as eating and playing. That it is complicated – whatever the details – is enough for Wittgenstein's purposes, as it precludes the idea that a child learns these things only by having something "occur in the mind" or by having "characteristic experiences."

For our purposes, the central passage in this stretch of remarks is the following:

> One attends to the shape, sometimes by tracing it, sometimes by screwing up one's eyes so as not to see the colour clearly, and so forth. I want to say: this and similar things are what one does *while* one 'directs one's attention to this or that.' But it isn't only these things that make us say that someone is attending to the shape, the colour, etc. Just as making a move in chess doesn't consist only in pushing a piece from here to there on the board – nor yet in thoughts and feelings that accompany the move: but in the circumstances that we call "playing a game of chess," "solving a chess problem," and the like. (PI, § 33)

The passage serves to close § 33 and refers back both to the discussion within the remark of the many different activities wherein attending to something's color might figure – mixing paints; noting the change in weather; trying to get a good look at something's color; asking after the name of a particular shade; and so on – as well as § 31's discussion of pointing to and explaining chess pieces in various circumstances. Wittgenstein's "it isn't only these things" announces the key point, upon which the chess example then elaborates. Although moves in chess happen – and happen at the moment – when players move pieces "from here to there on the board," those movements being – or counting as – moves involves more than this (and more than what players are thinking at the moment of moving the piece). To be a move, the movement of pieces has to be within a game of chess (or in such activities as demonstrating moves in chess, reconstructing a segment of a game of chess, and the like). Taken in isolation from those surroundings, the movements of such figures – like the lever and rod – could mean anything or nothing.

3.3 The Whole Hurly-Burly

The opening passages we have been considering lay the groundwork for many of the most important discussions later in the *Investigations*, including the discussion of *understanding*, which casts suspicion on its being a mental process; of *rule-following*, whose lesson is summarized at § 199: "To follow a rule, to make a report, to give an order, to play a game of chess, are *customs* (uses, institutions)"; and the so-called *private language argument* in the 200s, where the reminder that "much must be prepared in the language for mere naming to make sense" (PI, § 257) figures prominently. Rather than try to work these connections out further – doing so would take us too far afield – I want instead to look beyond the *Investigations* to note other points in Wittgenstein's later work where the kinds of ideas we have been considering are further developed.

There are numerous places in Wittgenstein's late writings where he emphasizes the situated character of language and thought within a broader, living
whole that is itself only indefinitely contoured. Consider:

> Only in the stream of thought and life do words have meaning. (RPP II,
> § 504)

> If a concept depends on a pattern of life, then there must be some indefinite-
> ness in it. For if a pattern deviates from the norm, what we want to say here
> would become quite dubious. (RPP II, § 652)

> Our concepts, judgements, reactions never appear in connection with just
> a single action, but rather with the whole swirl of human actions. (LW II,
> p. 56)[41]

> Seeing life as a weave, this pattern (pretence, say) is not always complete and
> is varied in a multiplicity of ways. But we, in our conceptual world, keep on
> seeing the same, recurring with variations. That is how our concepts take it.
> For concepts are not for use on a single occasion. (Z, § 568)

> A facial expression that was completely fixed couldn't be a friendly one.
> Variability and irregularity are essential to a friendly expression. Irregularity
> is part of its physiognomy (RPP II, § 615).

The last of these – from TS 232 from the late 1940s – appears shortly before
a sequence of remarks that reflects on and develops further his ideas about
situatedness, indeterminacy, and indefiniteness. The sequence runs from RPP II,
§ 622 to § 629. Although there is not a sharp break at that point, the consideration of themes this sequence announces and explores continues interspersed
after this stretch with a variety of cases and examples: feigning pain, the verb
"believe," and the desire to say things along the lines of "Who knows what is
going on inside him!" The sequence begins with the introduction of the para-
digmatic example of a vague concept – the concept of a *heap* – about which
Wittgenstein asks: "'Heap of sand' is a concept without sharp boundaries – but
why isn't one with sharp boundaries used instead of it? – Is the reason to be
found in the nature of the heaps? What phenomenon is it whose nature
determines our concept?" (RPP II, § 622).

Imagine having separate names – and so separate concepts – for heaps of sand
in accordance with the precise number of grains the heaps comprise. So a heap
with 18,324 grains of sand would be called by a different name – would fall
under a separate concept – than either a heap with 18,323 or 18,325 grains of
sand. Imagine trying to *use* these concepts. First of all, none of us could take in
at a glance – or even with considerable effort – the differences across heaps that

---

[41] In the typescript that serves as the basis of this volume, this remark is crossed out.

this series of concepts is meant to reflect. I cannot tell just by looking whether a heap has 18,323 or 18,324 grains of sand in it and I am not even remotely confident that I could differentiate them after considerable effort: not only do I not want to spend that much time *counting* grains of sand, but even if I tried, I would likely lose track – or lose interest – well before getting to the last grain.

The problems with such concepts run deeper than just our discriminatory capacities. Despite their initial appearance of sharpness and precision, applying these concepts in practice actually recapitulates rather than elim- inates the vagueness of the original concept of a *heap*. Suppose I am confronted with a pile of sand on a beach and suppose further that I have the wherewithal and determination to count the grains of sand making up the pile. At what point have I counted *all the grains* so that I can determine which of my more precise heap-like concepts applies? If the pile of sand is resting on and surrounded by more sand – as often happens with such piles, especially at the beach – which grains of sand *belong* to the pile rather than its surroundings? Do I have any principled way of determining whether a given grain of sand near or along the base or bottom of the pile belongs to the pile rather than the surroundings? Even if we imagine more idealized cases, where the heaps of sand sit atop sheets of glass or the like, there are still likely to be grains that are *borderline* in terms of belonging to the pile rather than being stray grains on the surrounding surface. And even if we had very precisely calibrated scales that are sensitive to the addition or subtrac- tion of one grain of sand, such scales would only differentiate between different *quantities of sand* without necessarily determining whether one or another of our more precisely defined heap-like concepts should be applied. Such thoughts suggest the *unnaturalness* of heap-like concepts that aspire to such precision; as he notes later in the sequence of remarks: "It is unnatural to draw a conceptual boundary line where there is not some special justification for it, where similarities would constantly draw us across the arbitrarily drawn line" (RPP II, § 628). Heaps or piles of sand differing only by one grain are about as similar as one can get and there is no real reason to try to differentiate among them in a, well, fine-grained way. Returning to Wittgenstein's questions, we can see that the difficulties of using or applying the concepts we are imagining as more precise than our familiar concept of a heap stem both from what we might attribute to *our nature* – our capacities for discriminating among different heaps, counting individual grains of sand, and so on – *and* what we might think of as belonging to the "nature of the heaps." What "determines our concept" of a heap spans the two.

Wittgenstein breaks off from considering the concept of a *heap* at this point and pivots to questions concerning behavior: "'A dog is more like a human being than a being endowed with a human form, but which behaved "mechanically."' Behaved according to simple rules?" (RPP II, § 623). We generally think and talk quite fluently about dogs even though their range of expression and patterns of activity are in many ways simpler and more limited[42] than is the case of human beings and even though they cannot *tell* us things in the myriad ways our fellow humans can. Dogs behave in a fluid and dynamic manner that both animates but also sometimes confounds our judgments regarding what they are up to or how they are faring. A more mechanically behaving being – even if "endowed with a human form" – would in one sense be easier to "read" in that its transitions from one state to another would be more precisely delineated, but those precise delineations would at the same time make the applicability of our concepts more difficult. We would not see what this being displays as expressive in the same way that we see even a dog's behavior as expressive. Wittgenstein notes this difficulty a few remarks later in our sequence: "Variability itself is a characteristic of behaviour without which behaviour would be to us as something completely different. (The facial features characteristic of grief, for instance, are not more meaningful than their mobility.)" (RPP II, §627).

An otherwise human-looking being whose facial expressions snapped from one to another as though turning a click-wheel and which displayed no subtle variations or nuance such that one expression shaded off so as to gradually merge with another would not strike us as expressive in a way that accommodated our usual concepts of grief, joy, sadness, distress, and the like. Such a being's expressions would perhaps strike us as caricatures or parodies of human expressions. By contrast, there is nothing parodic about a dog's growl or whine.

The key remarks in this sequence are the three that appear between Wittgenstein's remark about dogs and his appeal to the importance of the variability and mobility of facial expressions. There is also a fourth remark that appears after he remarks on arbitrarily drawn boundaries but fits thematically more with the three consecutive remarks than with what immediately precedes it. Here is the first passage: "We judge an action according to its background within human life, and this background is not monochrome, but we might picture it as a very complicated filigree pattern, which, to be sure, we can't copy, but which we can recognize from the general impression it makes" (RPP II, § 624).

---

[42] Although dogs are in some ways far *less* limited: consider their sense of hearing and especially their sense of smell. Dogs are able to locate items by scent in ways that no human being can.

Note the affinity of this remark with the closing paragraph of PI, § 33. Wittgenstein's remark there about what a move in chess consists in accords with his appeal here to a *background* against which we judge an action as the kind of action it is. Someone raises her hand. What action is that? Place that action in the setting of a classroom, and we will judge the action as indicating a desire to ask a question. On a busy city street, the action might be one of waving to a friend or hailing a cab. The "background within human life" is above all *complicated*: the background against which we judge actions has myriad elements (think of everything involved in a space's being a classroom) that make only a general impression.[43] There is no one way in which a classroom must be configured to serve as the backdrop for a raised hand. Classrooms come in all manner of sizes and layouts (think of lecture halls, seminar rooms, kindergarten classes, outdoor classrooms, and so on).

Wittgenstein's subsequent remarks in this sequence emphasize this kind of indeterminate complexity:

> The background is the bustle of life. And our concept points to something within *this* bustle. (RPP II, § 625)

> And it is the very concept "bustle" that brings about this indefiniteness. For a bustle comes about only through constant repetition. And there is no definite starting point for "constant repetition." (RPP II, § 626)

That this background is an indefinite bustle explains why it makes a general impression without our being able to copy it. To copy it would require delineating its elements and patterns in some precise way – line by line as it were – but doing so would transform what was being copied from background to foreground. What appears in the copy would no longer make a general impression but would be a precise drawing of something or other. The action we are judging would no longer stand out in the right way. There is perhaps another way to think of copying this indefinite bustle by creating a picture that was itself indefinite in various ways (through blur, shading, partial rendering, etc.). This would be more faithful to the kind of impression the background makes on us, but notice that there would be no one copy that "gets it right" about the background, as it could be indefinitely rendered in indefinitely many ways. In the final passage I want to emphasize, which appears just after the consecutive trio of remarks, Wittgenstein again invokes this idea of a background in a way that emphasizes its jumbled, indefinite character:

---

[43] For further discussion of Wittgenstein's appeal to a *background*, see Boncompagni (2014) and chapter 5 of Boncompagni (2016). See also Cerbone (2019a).

"How could human behavior be described? Surely only by showing the actions of a variety of humans, as they are all mixed up together. Not what *one* man is doing *now*, but the whole hurly-burly, is the background against which we see an action, and it determines our judgment, our concepts, and our reactions" (RPP II, § 629).[44]

Wittgenstein's appeals in these passages to such notions as "background," "filigree pattern," "bustle," and "the whole hurly-burly" weave together and serve to emphasize the three ideas I delineated in the opening passages of the *Investigations*: language as indefinitely open-ended and as a natural historical phenomenon, along with the rejection of what I referred to previously as an isolationist conception of meaning. Just how these ideas bear upon realism and idealism, which, in keeping with their almost complete disappearance in the later writings, have been absent from the discussion of this section so far, must now be considered.

3.4 The Persistence of Idealism

In *The View from Nowhere*, Thomas Nagel labels Wittgenstein "one of the most important sources of contemporary idealism" (1989, 105). Nagel is not alone in this assessment. Readers of Wittgenstein as diverse as David Bloor and Ernest Gellner interpret him as espousing a kind of culturally relativistic idealism.[45] Gellner does so in a more scathing manner, seeing Wittgenstein's views as benighted at best but mostly as pernicious. Bloor, by contrast, applauds Wittgenstein's enlightened turn toward a kind of sociology-first perspective, even if he did not carry out the kind of empirical research his views serve to found.[46] Other readings of Wittgenstein resist attributing to him a commitment to relativism, pernicious or enlightened, while nonetheless seeing in his later work a kind of idealism, a transcendental rather than an empirical or socially pluralistic form. Jonathan Lear's work on Wittgenstein – building on an essay by Bernard Williams – exemplifies this latter tendency in Wittgenstein interpretation.[47] Why is it that readers of the later work – some more careful than others – come away with the impression that his philosophy *must* ultimately be a kind of idealism?

Consider the following passage from MS-173, written in 1950 and published in *Remarks on Colour*:

> Would it be correct to say our concepts reflect (*spiegelt*) our life?
> They stand in the middle of it. (RC, § 302)

---

[44] This last remark also appears as Z, § 567.   [45] See Bloor (1983, 1996) and Gellner (1998).
[46] See Cerbone (1994) for a discussion of Bloor's characterization of Wittgenstein as a somewhat lazy sociologist.
[47] See Williams (1981), Lear (1982), and Lear and Stroud (1984).

Although the second sentence is clearly offered as a response to the initial question, the extent to which it affirms or rejects the correctness of what the first sentence asks after is not at all clear. The second sentence is offered without an explicitly affirmative or negative marker, which allows it to be read as suggesting either of the two:

> Would it be correct to say our concepts reflect our life?
>   Yes, by standing in the middle of it.

Or:

> Would it be correct to say our concepts reflect our life?
>   No, but they stand in the middle of it.

None of the idealist readings I am aware of cites this passage, but I think they can in all their varieties be understood as interpreting Wittgenstein's response to this query in the first manner, as affirming the correctness of this idea of reflection. When, for example, Nagel writes that for Wittgenstein, "nothing can make sense which purports to reach beyond the outer bounds of human experience and life" (105), this accords with the idea of our concepts reflecting or mirroring our lives: if our concepts *reflect* our lives, then they do not – and cannot – in any way get beyond them. Our lives circumscribe our concepts through this kind of mirror play, thereby setting boundaries against which our concepts rebound, as it were, like rays of light hitting a mirror.

Gellner clearly sees Wittgenstein as committed to this kind of mirroring, seeing in his philosophy a "communal-cultural vision of thought" that he uses "to solve or dissolve abstract problems of knowledge, to proclaim that they do not really arise, that our customary thought processes stand before no bar, face no indictment, have no case to answer" (Gellner, 1998, 77). As Gellner reads Wittgenstein, his aim in his later philosophy was to dissolve "the problem of the validation of our thought styles, our habits of reasoning and inference" via a "profoundly populist" method (Gellner, 1998, 77). For Wittgenstein, on this reading, "our conceptual customs are valid precisely because they are parts of a cultural custom. It is not merely the case that no other validation is available: no other validation is either possible or necessary. The very pursuit of such extra-cultural validation is the error of thought" (Gellner, 1998, 77). On this view, "custom is all we have, all we can have, and all we need" (Gellner, 1998, 77). That what Gellner refers to as "extra-cultural validation" is neither possible nor necessary accords with affirmation of the idea that our concepts reflect our lives: how could, on this model, there be anything beyond our lives that might serve to validate or invalidate what we think?

While Lear's transcendental reading eschews the kind of crude "village green" reading of Wittgenstein Gellner offers, his reading still ultimately endorses an affirmation of reflection or mirroring. Lear reads Wittgenstein as exploring what Lear refers to as our "mindedness" and its role in determining the sense of what we think and say. In parallel with Kant, Lear thinks Wittgenstein can be read as offering a kind of transcendental deduction, except that instead of the attachability of the "I think ... " to judgments or assertions, Wittgenstein argues for the attachment of "We are so minded ... " All judgments are implicitly reflections of our mindedness on this model. So far, this may sound like a recapitulation of Gellner's relativistic, "communal-cultural" understanding of Wittgenstein. Where Lear's reading differs from Gellner's lies in its *transcendental* understanding of the role our mindedness plays in constituting our judgments. The "We are so minded ... " ultimately drops out – or *disappears* – on Lear's reading, not because that prefix turns out not to be attachable – it always is – but because there are no contrasting forms of mindedness the prefix serves to exclude. Whereas Gellner's reading allows – and encourages – the idea of a plurality of cultures or communities, Lear's Wittgenstein endeavors to show that "the possibility of persons who are minded in any way at all is the possibility of their being minded as we are" (Lear 1982, 386). While Lear acknowledges that "it is only because we are minded as we are" that "we see the world the way we do," this does not "express an empirical truth"; it does not delineate "one possibility among others." Thus, for Lear's Wittgenstein, the following counterfactual:

If we were other-minded, we would see the world differently

"must be nonsense" (Lear 1982, 392). Although a radical departure from the likes of Gellner and Bloor's cultural relativism, Lear's transcendental turn serves only to intensify the reflective relation between our life and our concepts, as the very idea of anything's reaching beyond them is excluded in principle.

Given our discussion in our lead-up to considering idealist readings of the later work, that Wittgenstein says that our concepts "stand in the middle" of our life should be entirely unsurprising. Whether we look to the opening remarks of the *Investigations* or to his appeals to the "hurly-burly" that serve as "background" to our actions or judgments, what he says in the *Remarks on Colour* passage fully accords with his rejection of the kind of magical isolationism he targets in the *Investigations*. That accordance can, however, be understood without committing Wittgenstein to an endorsement of the idea of *reflection* that fuels idealist readings. Reading Wittgenstein's response to the queried correctness of the idea of reflection as affirming that idea conflates the *conditions* for a concept's application – for a concept of

whatever kind being in play – with the *content* of the concept.[48] It is one thing
to note the way something only counts as, variously, an action, a gesture, an
utterance, the application of a concept – a move in a game – only against the
wider backdrop of human activity – actions, gestures, utterances, and so on
"all mixed up together" – but quite another to say that what such things are
about pertains to that wider backdrop.

To see that Wittgenstein is careful to make this distinction, consider the flow
of remarks toward the end of Part VI of *Remarks on the Foundations of
Mathematics*, whose forty-nine remarks are taken from MS-164 from the
early to mid-1940s. At § 41, Wittgenstein characteristically remarks: "Only in
the practice of a language can a word have meaning." And slightly thereafter:
"Language just is a phenomenon of human life" (RFM VI, § 47). So again we
see the kinds of ideas I've emphasized throughout this section, but we can add
a further one that concerns the kind of *agreement* the ongoing practice of
language involves and requires: sustaining a practice – of following a rule,
applying a concept, speaking meaningfully – depends upon a kind of ongoing
agreement in terms of how up-and-coming language users respond to training,
carry on from examples, react to correction, and so on. Wittgenstein refers to
this here – as he does in the *Investigations* (see PI, § 242) – as "agreement in
judgments," which serves to found and sustain our ongoing practices. He asks:
"Suppose one day instruction no longer produced agreement?" followed by,
"Could there be arithmetic without agreement on the part of calculators?" (RFM
VI, § 45). Wittgenstein does not directly or explicitly answer these questions,
but they encourage us to consider how much must be in place – and be taken for
granted – in the imparting of even simple arithmetical formulas. If everyone's
"natural reactions" diverged wildly from one another, if everyone carried on
differently from a given set of examples, and if everyone reacted to correction in
different and unpredictable ways, then the practice of doing sums, developing
series of numbers, and so on would break down. Hence the importance of these
myriad conditions that resist any kind of definite enumeration. But it does not
follow that what we understand when we understand arithmetic or basic logical
patterns – when we say "3 + 6 = 9," for example, or that q follows from p and *If
p, then q* – is in some way *about* those indefinitely enumerable forms of
agreement that pervade the hurly-burly against which we say such things. The
closing remark is unambiguous on this point:

---

[48] Bloor (1991) is guilty of that kind of conflation, especially if one extrapolates from his reading of
Frege. For Bloor, Frege's famous antipsychologism about logic leaves room for a kind of
sociologism, such that the *content* of logic (and mathematics) is socially inflected. I discuss
Bloor's views on content in Cerbone (2015).

What you say seems to amount to this, that logic belongs to the natural history of man. And that is not combinable with the hardness of the logical "must."

But the logical "must" is a component part of the propositions of logic, and these are not propositions of human natural history. If what a proposition of logic said was: Human beings agree with one another in such and such ways (and that would be the form of the natural-historical proposition), then its contradictory would say that there is here a *lack* of agreement. Not, that there is agreement of another kind.

The agreement of humans that is a presupposition of logic is not an agreement in *opinions*, much less in opinions on questions of logic. (RFM VI, § 49)

Wittgenstein's appeals to the "bustle of life" and the "whole hurly-burly" bear upon idealist readings beyond the question of how "stand in the middle" affirms or corrects the idea of reflection. Idealist readings ignore two crucial aspects of Wittgenstein's talk of our concepts as standing in the middle of our lives: first, that our lives take place within a broader *world* that involves the obtaining of various ranges of facts and, second, that "our life" is ongoing and indefinitely bounded. Neither of these ideas comports especially well with idealism. To start with the first, we have seen how Wittgenstein's conception of life – our life, our form of life – becomes increasingly naturalistic as we head into the later period. Language is a natural historical phenomenon, just like our eating, walking, and so on. Seeing language as a natural historical phenomenon involves seeing language as operative within a broader setting of human activity – in keeping with the sense of "language-games" I've been emphasizing – and that human activity is itself situated within a broader environing world. What pertains to language – and what pertains to our "mindedness" – includes *facts*: facts about our natural history; facts about our capacities and sensibilities; but also facts about the way the things are in the world around us (the persistence and stability of objects; the manner in which properties and groups of properties are instantiated; and so on). There is not a *something* – call it our life, language, or mindedness – that can be delineated and considered apart from the world to which it belongs. Insofar as our life is always backgrounded by a hurly-burly – insofar as it is situated within a bustle – it already belongs to a world that exceeds it.

At the same time, we can imagine those facts being otherwise, and this helps us to get a grip on the idea of there being other ways of making sense of things – other concepts – even if we cannot quite get a grip on what it would be like to have those concepts. As Wittgenstein notes in the fragment that accompanies the more polished remarks of the *Investigations*:

I am not saying: if such-and-such facts of nature were different, people would have different concepts (in the sense of a hypothesis). Rather: if anyone believes that certain concepts are absolutely the correct ones, and that having

> different ones would mean not realizing something that we realize – then let
> him imagine certain very general facts of nature to be different from what we
> are used to, and the formation of concepts different from the usual ones will
> become intelligible to him. (PPF, § 366/PI II, § xii)

Wittgenstein's advice here does not comport well with the idea that he aims to
provide a kind of transcendental deduction whose conclusion is that what it is to
be minded at all is to be minded as we are.[49]

When Nagel writes that for Wittgenstein "nothing can make sense which
purports to reach beyond the outer bounds of human experience and life" (1989,
105) we should be suspicious, to say the least, of this talk of an "outer bounds,"
as it suggests that our life, language, or mindedness forms a kind of bounded
whole. Compare Wittgenstein's likening of "our language" to an ancient city,
which we considered earlier: the city's life is ongoing, with age-old mazes of
streets to which suburbs and thoroughfares have been added. While one can take
a kind of snapshot of the city at any given time, the city is at no point static or
complete: what borders or boundaries it has are temporary and contingent;
things that were "off limits" – or unthinkable – at some point in time might
later be pedestrian and matter of course (consider Wittgenstein's examples of
chemistry and calculus). The diversity of linguistic forms "is not something
fixed, given once for all; but new types of language, new language-games, as we
may say, come into existence, and others become obsolete and forgotten" (PI, §
23). How these developments have come about – how the ancient city came to
have "straight and regular streets and uniform houses"; why some neighbor-
hoods were demolished and replaced with something new; why hardly anyone
still frequents a particular quarter – is a long and complicated story replete with
insights, discoveries, practical pressures, political realignments, and so on.
Really, we should not think of it as *a* story at all, but a multitude of stories
whose details depend upon the "neighborhood" under consideration. That there
is such a multitude suggests that there is no one general way to describe or think
about *the* relation between language and thought – our lives in language – and
the world, which in turn suggests that there is nothing in the later Wittgenstein to
encourage a general thesis in the form of either realism or idealism.

4 Coda: Remarks on *On Certainty*

Wittgenstein died in April 1951. Over the course of the last eighteen months of
his life, he wrote a series of remarks whose impetus was G. E. Moore's several
defenses of common sense and accompanying proof for the existence of the

---

[49] This aspect of Lear's reading has been sharply criticized by Barry Stroud. See his contribution –
"The Allure of Idealism" – to Lear and Stroud (1984).

external world. The last of these remarks was composed just two days before his death. They were later published as a freestanding volume, *On Certainty*. As the volume's editors note, these notes are very much "first draft material, which he did not live to excerpt and polish" (OC, vi). That alone is reason to be guarded in terms of interpreting this material and assessing the ways in which it continues on – and diverges – from other later material.[50] A further reason emerges from examination of the content of these remarks, as Wittgenstein – prompted by the specifics of Moore's ideas – introduces a number of new ideas and images that do not have ready correlates in earlier work.[51] In these closing remarks, I will not offer anything like a "reading" of *On Certainty* as a whole (whatever exactly that means, given the status of the remarks). My aim here will only be to note the ways in which I see these last remarks as bearing upon realism and idealism, especially insofar as they provide new ways for thinking about the themes delineated thus far.

Consider the following remark from Wittgenstein's *On Certainty*: "But I did not get my picture of the world by satisfying myself of its correctness; nor do I have it because I am satisfied of its correctness. No: it is the inherited background against which I distinguish between true and false" (OC, § 94).

On Certainty here offers another characterization of a *background* against which our judgments are determined. Instead of a *hurly-burly*, Wittgenstein here appeals to "my picture of the world." Wittgenstein's bracketing here of questions concerning that picture's correctness accords with his suspicions of Moore's attempts to refute skepticism and defend "common sense." Moore's attempts involve adducing what he characterizes as commonplace pieces of knowledge – that *here is one hand*, for example – which may serve as premises for an argument whose conclusion contravenes the skeptic's questioning our knowing that there is an external world. What Wittgenstein finds puzzling about Moore's appeal to these commonplaces – what we might think of as elements of this inherited background – is his citing them as instances or examples of *knowledge*. That is, Wittgenstein contends that it is not at all clear just what Moore *means* when he says, holding up his hand, "I know that this is my hand" or, standing before a tree in the garden, "I know that this is a tree." It is not clear what the point of saying some such thing would be because it is not clear what it

---

[50] The wealth of archival material that attests to Wittgenstein's obsessive reworking and rearranging of his remarks further underscores that an abundance of caution is needed in interpreting *On Certainty*.

[51] See Moyal-Sharrock's introduction to Moyal-Sharrock and Brenner (2005) for an overview of the reception and significance of *On Certainty*. In contrast to the note of caution I've been sounding, in her estimation, the work stands as a third masterwork alongside the *Tractatus* and the *Investigations*, despite its rough and provisional status.

would mean to claim otherwise. There is no room for doubt in such cases, and so no room for such related notions as finding out, making sure, confirming, and disconfirming. Since I don't know what it would be like seriously to doubt – here and now – that, for example, I have two hands or that the earth's existence predates my own, then the sense of saying that I *do* know such things is attenuated at best. What Moore appeals to are *certainties*, but this would appear to exclude them from the "language-game" of knowing. Playing that game involves the possibility of making various kinds of "moves" – questioning, challenging, proving, disproving, and so on – that are not available when it comes to Moore's examples.

Moore's efforts to disarm the skeptic serve to draw our attention to the presence and role of such certainties with respect to what it *does* make sense to claim to know and doubt: "When Moore says he *knows* such and such, he is really enumerating a lot of empirical propositions which we affirm without special testing; propositions, that is, which have a peculiar logical role in the system of our empirical propositions" (OC, § 136).

Just how to characterize this "peculiar logical role" is a delicate – and controversial – matter, but we might start by saying something like this: what Moore is onto, whether he realizes it or not, is a range of things that everyone accepts – or we might say "just knows" – but without much (or anything) in the way of explicit instruction and certainly without any testing, investigating, or justifying. But even saying "everyone" is not quite right and for a number of reasons: first, what is accepted in this manner will vary from person to person. There are, for example, indexical elements involved in these propositions. One example that recurs throughout *On Certainty* is, "My name is Ludwig Wittgenstein," which is a certainty for Wittgenstein, but not for anyone else (unless they also happen to be named Ludwig Wittgenstein). Second, and more important, what individuals accept in this manner – what "holds fast" for them – varies depending on their "world picture," which is not at all uniform for everyone everywhere. There is thus a historical-cultural dimension to this kind of acceptance, such that different propositions will have this status for different peoples and at different times: "But what men consider reasonable or unreasonable alters. At certain periods men find reasonable what at other periods they found unreasonable. And vice versa" (OC, § 336). One thing this variation shows is that there is nothing *intrinsic* to these propositions that serves to explain their "peculiar logical role." Although Wittgenstein appeals to logic frequently in *On Certainty*, these propositions are at the same time empirical in form, so there is nothing like the notion of such propositions being tautologies or "analytic" at work here, nor any notion of these propositions being self-evident or irrefutable.

So what interests Wittgenstein is not a project of trying to delineate a determinate and unique set of privileged propositions – there is no such set[52] – but instead following out the idea that there must be *some such set* in order for there to be a life with epistemic concepts such as know, doubt, confirm, disconfirm, and so on. Wittgenstein illustrates this in mythological terms with his famous image of the riverbed in OC, §§ 96–99. In order for water to flow in definite directions, rather than slop any which way (an image of madness, perhaps), there must be a riverbed that serves to channel it. The riverbed need not have just one set of contours, but there must be some such bed. As a result, "One cannot make experiments if there are not some things that one does not doubt" (OC, § 337). As Wittgenstein notes shortly after this remark: "That is to say, the *questions* that we raise and our *doubts* depend on the fact that some propositions are exempt from doubt, are as it were like hinges on which those turn" (OC, § 341). " That is to say, it belongs to the logic of our scientific investigations that certain things are *in deed* not doubted" (OC, § 342).

The dependence Wittgenstein notes here is a kind of *logical* dependence. Wittgenstein appeals to logic in the one appearance of *realism* in the work: "'I know' is here a *logical* insight. Only realism can't be proved by means of it" (OC, § 59). Recall from our discussion of the middle-period Wittgenstein's insistence that "realism is always right in what it says" (MS-156b, 22 v). We can hear in this late passage a distant echo of that earlier idea: the realist is right insofar as there is no clear way of impugning assertions such as "I have hands" along the lines of an idealist's appeal to appearances. If my hands stopped "appearing" to me, I would very likely see this as indicating a problem about my *eyesight* rather than an occasion to doubt my having hands. At the same time, noting those many things that we "just know" does not amount to a *proof* of anything, except that we take for granted certain ways of talking and thinking. As Wittgenstein notes in the *Investigations*, the realist is only defending a "normal form of expression." Nothing further in terms of proving anything about what there is follows.

What works like hinges – hinge-propositions – are those things where being wrong is ruled out. Wittgenstein says as much in § 425 of *On Certainty*: "And this too is right: I cannot be making a *mistake* about it." However, he goes on to remark: "But that does not mean that I am infallible about it." As holding fast, hinge-propositions have this peculiar status of being immune from challenge or any kind of serious questioning, but without our being entitled, on the basis of

---

[52] This is a point emphasized in (Rhees, 2008). Indeed, Rhees refers to the idea that there is such a determinate set that Wittgenstein in *On Certainty* either tries to delineate or at the very least encourages us to try to determine as the "*most commonly* made" misunderstanding of the work.

such immunity, to assert their truth. I cannot take seriously the idea of being mistaken about any such hinge-proposition – that is what marks them out as *certainties* – but it does not (just like that) make sense to say that I *know* them. At the same time, these hinge-propositions make up the background – the *Weltbild* – that gives shape to my making sense of the world in ways that involve making inquiries, providing justification, possibly knowing, but also being mistaken.

That the picture of the world which functions as background is neither justified nor unjustified does not align well with realism insofar as realism seeks to infer how things are from what we find ourselves unable to doubt. At the same time, the ideas that Wittgenstein begins to sketch in *On Certainty* do not sit well with idealism either. In keeping with the trajectory we have been following throughout our discussion, a neither-nor attitude seems more warranted. That something – a picture of the world; hinge propositions; a framework – "holds fast" whenever we conduct any form of inquiry suggests again a rejection of a picture of the mind – or our mindedness – as something that can be isolated and delineated apart from an involvement with the world. "Our *acting* ... lies at the bottom of the language-game" (OC, § 204) and our activity is situated within – and responsive to – a broader social *and* natural world. Further reflection on Wittgenstein's river imagery encourages this idea of responsiveness. While a distinction at any time can be made between what is "hardened" and what is "fluid," and thus between what channels the water and the water that courses over the riverbed, Wittgenstein is careful to note that "there is not a sharp division of one from the other." The water is never entirely free of sediment and particulates that get pulled away from the bed, thereby altering and shifting the bed over time. There is thus a kind of reciprocal relationship between riverbed and the flowing water: the riverbed channels the water – makes there *be* a river at all – but the water shapes and shifts the riverbed over time. Wittgenstein makes this clear in less mythological terms later in the text:

> The child learns to believe a host of things. I.e. it learns to act according to these beliefs. Bit by bit there forms a system of what is believed, and in that system some things stand unshakeably and some are more or less liable to shift. What stands fast does so, not because it is intrinsically obvious or convincing; *it is rather held fast by what lies around it.* (OC, § 144 – my emphasis)

"What lies around it" are ordinary empirical propositions – assertions, questions, conjectures, hypotheses, and so on – all formed as part of our ordinary commerce in and with the world that includes everything from our most everyday ordinary activities to our farthest flung scientific research. These activities can be characterized as expressions of our mindedness as long this does not draw us toward making the kinds of divisions and distinctions that fuel the debate between realism and idealism. Much later in *On Certainty*, Wittgenstein writes: "You must bear in mind that the language-game is so to say something unpredictable. I mean: it is not based on grounds. It is not reasonable (or unreasonable). It is there – like our life" (OC, § 559).

Where else would *there* be but the world?

References

Primary Sources

BBB   *The Blue and Brown Books*. New York: Harper and Row, 1965.

BNE   Bergen Nachlass Edition (www.wittgensteinsource.org).

BT   *The Big Typescript: TS 213*. Edited and translated by C. G. Luckhardt and M. Aue. Oxford: Blackwell, 2005.

LW I   *Last Writings on the Philosophy of Psychology, Volume I*. Edited by G. H. von Wright and Heikki Nyman, translated by C. G. Luckhardt and M. A. E. Aue. Chicago: University of Chicago Press, 1982.

LW II   *Last Writings on the Philosophy of Psychology, Volume 2: The Inner and the Outer, 1949–1951*. Edited by G. H. von Wright and H. Nyman, translated by C. G. Luckhardt and M. Aue. Oxford: Blackwell, 1992.

NB   *Notebooks, 1914–1916*. 2nd edition. Translated by G. E. M. Anscombe. Chicago: University of Chicago Press, 1979.

OC   *On Certainty*. Edited by G. E. M. Anscombe and G. H. von Wright, translated by Denis Paul and G. E. M. Anscombe. New York: Harper and Row, 1969.

PG   *Philosophical Grammar*. Edited by R. Rhees, translated by A. Kenny. Oxford: Blackwell, 1974.

PI   *Philosophical Investigations*. 4th edition, revised. Edited by P. M. S. Hacker and J. Schulte, translated by G. E. M. Anscombe, P. M. S. Hacker, and J. Schulte. Oxford: Wiley-Blackwell, 2009.

PPF/PI-II   *Philosophy of Psychology: A Fragment*. Published with the 4th edition of the *Philosophical Investigations*. Previously published as Part Two in earlier editions.

PR   *Philosophical Remarks*. Edited by R. Rhees, translated by R. Hargreaves and R. White. Oxford: Basil Blackwell, 1975.

RC   *Remarks on Colour*. Edited by G. E. M. Anscombe, translated by L. McAlister and M. Schättle. Berkeley: University of California Press, 1977.

RFM   *Remarks on the Foundations of Mathematics*. Edited by G. H. von Wright, R. Rhees, and G. E. M. Anscombe, translated by G. E. M. Anscombe. Cambridge, MA: The Massachusetts Institute of Technology Press, 1978.

RPP II   *Remarks on the Philosophy of Psychology, Volume II*. Edited by G. H. von Wright and Heikki Nyman, translated by C. G. Luckhardt and M. A. E. Aue. Chicago: University of Chicago Press, 1980.

TLP   *Tractatus Logico-Philosophicus*. Translated by B. F. McGuinness and D. Pears. London: Routledge, 1961.

Z   *Zettel*. Edited by G. E. M. Anscombe and G. H. von Wright, translated by G. E. M. Anscombe. Berkeley: University of California Press, 1967.

Secondary Sources

Anscombe, G. E. M. (1981) "The Question of Linguistic Idealism." In *From Parmenides to Wittgenstein*. Oxford: Blackwell.

Bartmann, Marius (2021) *Wittgenstein's Metametaphysics and the Realism-Idealism Debate*. Basingstoke: Palgrave Macmillan.

Bloor, David (1983) *Wittgenstein: A Social Theory of Knowledge*. New York: Columbia University Press.

    (1991) *Knowledge and Social Imagery*. Chicago: University of Chicago Press.

    (1996) "The Question of Linguistic Idealism Revisited." In *The Cambridge Companion to Wittgenstein*, edited by H. Sluga and D. Stern. Cambridge: Cambridge University Press.

Boncompagni, Anna (2014) "On Trying to Say What 'Goes Without Saying': Wittgenstein on Certainty and Ineffability." *Journal of Theories and Research in Education* 9 (1): 51–68.

    (2015) "Elucidating Forms of Life: The Evolution of a Philosophical Tool." *Nordic Wittgenstein Review* 4: 155–175.

    (2016) *Wittgenstein and Pragmatism*. London: Palgrave Macmillan.

    (2022) *Wittgenstein on Forms of Life*. Cambridge: Cambridge University Press.

Cavell, Stanley (1990) *Conditions Handsome and Unhandsome*. Chicago: University of Chicago Press.

    (1995) "Notes and Afterthoughts on the Opening of Wittgenstein's *Investigations*." Pages 125–186 in *Philosophical Passages*. Oxford: Blackwell.

Cerbone, David R. (1994) "Don't Look But Think: Imaginary Scenarios in Wittgenstein's Later Philosophy." *Inquiry* 37 (2): 159–183.

    (2003) "The Limits of Conservatism: Wittgenstein on 'Our Life' and 'Our Concepts'." Pages 43–62 in *The Grammar of Politics*, edited by C. Heyes. Ithaca, NY: Cornell University Press.

(2015) "Wittgenstein and Idealism." Pages 311–332 in *The Oxford Handbook to Wittgenstein*, edited by M. McGinn and O. Kuusela. Oxford: Oxford University Press.

(2019a) "Ground, Background, and Rough Ground: Dreyfus, Wittgenstein, and Phenomenology." Pages 62–79 in *Normativity, Meaning, and the Promise of Phenomenology*, edited by M. Burch, J. Marsh, and I. McMullin. New York: Routledge.

(2019b) "'Life Is Very Complicated': Remarks on a Recurring Adjective." Pages 135–149 in *Wittgensteinian (Adj.)*, edited by S. Wuppuluri and N. da Costa. New York: Springer.

(2020) "Unruly Readers, Unruly Words: Wittgenstein and Language." Pages 624–645 in *The Cambridge History of Philosophy, 1945–2015*, edited by K. Becker and I. Thomson. Cambridge: Cambridge University Press.

Cockburn, David (2021) *Wittgenstein, Conversation and Human Beings*. London: Anthem Press.

Diamond, Cora (1991) *The Realistic Spirit*. Cambridge, MA: Massachusetts Institute of Technology Press.

Friedlander, Eli (2001) *Signs of Sense: Reading Wittgenstein's* Tractatus. Cambridge, MA: Harvard University Press.

Gellner, Ernest (1998) *Language and Solitude: Wittgenstein, Malinowski, and the Hapsburg Dilemma*. Cambridge: Cambridge University Press.

Goldfarb, Warren (1983) "I Want You to Bring Me a Slab: Remarks on the Opening Sections of the *Philosophical Investigations*." *Synthese* 56 (3): 265–282.

Ishiguro, Hidé (1969) "Use and Reference of Names." Pages 20–50 in *Studies in the Philosophy of Wittgenstein*, edited by P. Winch. London: Routledge and Kegan Paul.

Lear, Jonathan (1982) "Leaving the World Alone." *The Journal of Philosophy* 79 (7): 382–403.

Lear, Jonathan, and Stroud, Barry (1984) "The Disappearing 'We'." *Proceedings of the Aristotelian Society Supplemental Volumes* 58: 219–258.

McDowell, John (1984) "Wittgenstein on Following a Rule." *Synthese* 58 (March): 325–364.

(1996) *Mind and World*. Cambridge, MA: Harvard University Press.

McGuinness, Brian (1981) "The So-Called Realism of Wittgenstein's *Tractatus*." Pages 60–73 in *Perspectives on the Philosophy of Wittgenstein*, edited by I. Block. Oxford: Basil Blackwell.

McManus, Denis (2006) *The Enchantment of Words: Wittgenstein's* Tractatus Logico-Philosophicus. New York: Oxford University Press.

(2012) *Heidegger and the Measure of Truth*. Oxford: Oxford University Press.

Moore, Adrian William, and Sullivan, Peter (2003) "Ineffability and Nonsense." *Proceedings of the Aristotelian Society Supplemental Volumes* 77: 169–193 and 195–223.

Moore, G. E. (1959) *Philosophical Studies*. Paterson, NJ: Littlefield, Adams, and Company.

Mounce, Howard Owen (1997) "Philosophy, Solipsism and Thought." *The Philosophical Quarterly* 47 (186): 1–18.

Moyal-Sharrock, Daniele, and Brenner, William (2005) *Readings of Wittgenstein's* On Certainty. Basingstoke: Palgrave Macmillan.

Nagel, Thomas (1989) *The View from Nowhere*. Oxford: Oxford University Press.

Proops, Ian (2000) *Logic and Language in Wittgenstein's* Tractatus. New York: Routledge.

Rhees, Rush (2008) *Wittgenstein's* On Certainty*: There – Like Our Life*. Edited by D. Z. Phillips. Oxford: Wiley-Blackwell.

(2015) "Wittgenstein's Philosophical Conversations with Rush Rhees (1939–50): From the Notes of Rush Rhees." Edited by G. Citron. *Mind* 124 (403): 1–71.

Richter, Duncan (2022) *Wittgenstein's* Tractatus*: A Student's Edition*. Lanham, MD: Lexington Books.

Ritter, Bernhard (2020) *Kant and Post-Tractarian Wittgenstein: Transcendentalism, Idealism, Illusion*. Basingstoke, UK: Palgrave Macmillan.

Russell, Bertrand (1959) *The Problems of Philosophy*. New York: Oxford University Press.

Stern, David (1995) *Wittgenstein on Mind and Language*. Oxford: Oxford University Press.

(2018) "Introduction." Pages 1–24 in *Wittgenstein in the 1930s: Between the* Tractatus *and the* Investigations, edited by D. Stern. Cambridge: Cambridge University Press.

Stroud, Barry (2002) *Meaning, Understanding, and Practice: Philosophical Papers*. Oxford: Oxford University Press.

Sullivan, Peter (1996) "The 'Truth' in Solipsism, and Wittgenstein's Rejection of the A Priori." *European Journal of Philosophy* 4 (2): 195–220.

(2001) "A Version of the Picture Theory." Pages 89–110 in *Ludwig Wittgenstein*: Tractatus logico-philosophicus, edited by W. Vossenkuhl. Berlin: Akademie Verlag.

Williams, Bernard (1981) "Wittgenstein and Idealism." Pages 144–163 in *Moral Luck: Philosophical Papers 1973–1980*. Cambridge: Cambridge University Press.

Acknowledgments

I would like to thank Maria Balaska, Filippo Casati, Henry Cerbone, Randall Havas, and Ed Minar, as well as an anonymous referee, for comments, criticism, and discussion of earlier drafts of this Element. I would also like to thank David Stern for his many comments and suggestions, as well as for shepherding this project through to completion.

Cambridge Elements ≡

The Philosophy of Ludwig Wittgenstein

David G. Stern

University of Iowa

David G. Stern is a Professor of Philosophy and a Collegiate Fellow in the College of Liberal Arts and Sciences at the University of Iowa. His research interests include history of analytic philosophy, philosophy of language, philosophy of mind, and philosophy of science. He is the author of *Wittgenstein's Philosophical Investigations: An Introduction* (Cambridge University Press, 2004) and *Wittgenstein on Mind and Language* (Oxford University Press, 1995), as well as more than 50 journal articles and book chapters. He is the editor of *Wittgenstein in the 1930s: Between the 'Tractatus' and the 'Investigations'* (Cambridge University Press, 2018) and is also a co-editor of the *Cambridge Companion to Wittgenstein* (Cambridge University Press, 2nd edition, 2018), *Wittgenstein: Lectures, Cambridge 1930–1933, from the Notes of G. E. Moore* (Cambridge University Press, 2016) and *Wittgenstein Reads Weininger* (Cambridge University Press, 2004).

About the Series

This series provides concise and structured introductions to all the central topics in the philosophy of Ludwig Wittgenstein. The Elements are written by distinguished senior scholars and bright junior scholars with relevant expertise, producing balanced and comprehensive coverage of the full range of Wittgenstein's thought.

Cambridge Elements ^Ξ

The Philosophy of Ludwig Wittgenstein

Printed in the USA
CPSIA information can be obtained
at www.ICGtesting.com
LVHW011108250124
769704LV00003B/206